ACT LIKE YOU'RE HAVING A GOOD TIME

MICHELE WELDON

✫ ACT ✫ LIKE YOU'RE HAVING ✫ A GOOD TIME ✫

ESSAYS

NORTHWESTERN UNIVERSITY PRESS

EVANSTON, ILLINOIS

Northwestern University Press
www.nupress.northwestern.edu

Printed in the United States of America

10 9 8 7 6 5 4 3 2 1

Library of Congress Cataloging-in-Publication Data
Names: Weldon, Michele, 1958– author.
Title: Act like you're having a good time : essays / Michele Weldon.
Description: Evanston, Illinois : Northwestern University Press, 2020.
Identifiers: LCCN 2020020817 | ISBN 9780810142947 (paperback) |
   ISBN 9780810142954 (ebook)
Subjects: LCSH: Weldon, Michele, 1958– | Weldon, Michele, 1958–
   —Family. | Women journalists—United States—Biography.
Classification: LCC CT275.W3785 A5 2020 | DDC 070.92—dc23
LC record available at https://lccn.loc.gov/2020020817

*For Mama Pat and Papa Bill
and my three wise men,
Weldon, Brendan, and Colin*

Women have often felt insane when cleaving the truth of our experience. Our future depends on the sanity of each of us and we have a profound stake beyond the personal, in the project of describing our reality as candidly and fully as we can to each other.

—Adrienne Rich

CONTENTS

PART THREE. MEANING

INTRODUCTION

"ACT LIKE YOU'RE HAVING A GOOD TIME."

My father would say this to the six of us—Mary Pat, Maureen, Bill, Madeleine, Paul, and me—alone or in a group, likely when we were in the white Chrysler station wagon with the luggage rack, with Dad driving as my mother sat in the front passenger seat, her bucket purse at her feet.

Dad offered this admonition calmly if we complained, fought with each other, or gave him or my mother a hard time, refusing to do what was indeed not optional. Most of my parents' behavioral requirements—I did not say requests—involved us doing chores or going to an event, family party, dinner, school meeting, or whatever was on the calendar and not open to refusal. The hashtag for my parents' approach to our childhoods—had there been hashtags in the '50s, '60s, and '70s—would have been #NotAnOption.

Swallow your resistance and reservations and oblige. You might as well smile.

Most often Dad was affable, pleasant. He delivered this mandate not as a superficial "Fake it until you make it" declaration. His mantra was about demanding we rise above the daily pettiness that consumed us.

Those activities included back-and-forth nonsense bickering over who ate the last brownie, drank the last Pepsi, touched or moved a favorite (fill in the blank)—all demonstrating the entrenched stubbornness we bore for the heck of it. There were the territorial wars ("I called it first!") over who got the best pillow on the floor in the basement to watch TV, or just the "I'd rather not" response we gave to a lot of what we were expected to do.

"Do we have to?"

"Yes."

My father was not so interested in a lot of back-and-forth. Discussion and interpretation were not on the agenda. He just wanted to move ahead and proceed calmly without conflagration or conflict. Dad was not a talkative guy, nor was he indulgent. We knew we had no hardship. He just wanted to make sure we knew and acted accordingly.

I wish I had his smooth and endearing temperament. I don't; admittedly, I am more like my mother. I see her particularly in my declarations and calling out everything "as I see it," which at times is unapologetic and forthright. I have been called "difficult"—a frequent indictment of women who speak their minds. "Spirited," they say now if they are not trying too hard to insult you. It is intended as the immediate erasure of likability. Those are the cutting remarks that show up on your feedback forms, in HR sessions, during job interviews, or at talkbacks when you are given the promotion and the raise in spite of your directness. The assignment of this label always comes with an implicit warning to be quiet, don't rock the boat.

I also have been described as having "a big personality," which is code for women who say what they think, express ambition, and show an intolerance for systems and their enforcers that are biased, unjust, and limiting. I have a lot of good company in that club.

A lot of times the follow-up to my father's directive for acting pleasant was, "Don't be a Gloomy Gus." That was something I thought only people in my family knew because I never heard it anywhere else. I later learned that Gus was a cartoon character from the 1930s, sort of like Debbie Downer was generations later on *Saturday Night Live*.

My father was right about most things, but particularly about presenting an amicable demeanor. Headed to rehearsal for an Oak Park–River Forest High School play (where I was only in the chorus that one time for *Oliver!*), or cheerleading for a Hardey Prep football game when it was bitter cold, I learned that his admonition to try to find pleasantries in a task usually kicked in. Just attempting to enjoy something transformed into the notion not only that it wasn't so bad, but most times whatever I had rallied against so fervently was enjoyable, if not altogether brief and over soon enough. Simple, useful advice that mostly worked.

Of course, this didn't erase every minor inconvenience or twist of fate, in childhood and throughout life, but it tempered the disappointment.

Fifty years before finding your bliss was a thing, my father reminded us bliss was a choice and within our reach. Long before "Just do it" was a Nike mantra, my father nudged us to live our lives that way—not with blind obedience but with an intended optimism. I am grateful to him for steering us in that direction because while highly simplistic, it is not a bad way to go about your life. His words still help me, particularly at networking gatherings, meetings, or parties where my attendance is a must and where it all seems a bit off-kilter.

"Act like you're having a good time."

People want to be around you if you are happy. *You* want to be around you. You can also get way more done; succumbing to elective negativity tends to slow everything down.

I SET UP MY PORTABLE EASEL, AT TIMES STRUGGLING TO GET the tripod legs the right height and to secure the 12-by-16-inch canvas to the easel in case it is a windy day. I search for the duct tape in one of my many canvas totes.

The last three summers I have taken a plein air oil painting class eight Saturdays in a row, with makeups offered for rain-outs. We stay at one location for two weeks straight because you can't finish a painting in one session. Often those four or five hours painting at Twelfth Street Beach or the Garden of the Phoenix in Jackson Park were for me the best part of that week.

A band of six to eight of us amateur artists arrive at the designated spot every Saturday, about 9:00 or 10:00 a.m., depending on when everyone agrees it is best. We meet our instructor, Laura Mueller, whom we all first met in sketch classes when she was an instructor at the Art Institute of Chicago.

She sends emails each week to the group explaining the assignment, what artists' techniques we will be exploring—whether it is Claude Lorrain, the seventeenth-century landscape artist, or Jean-Baptiste-Camille Corot, the nineteenth-century painter whose seascapes exude a dreamlike essence. Yes, we also strain to imitate Paul Cézanne and John Singer Sargent, knowing that we also need to navigate it all in a few hours on a Saturday. Laura sends us resources to study before we arrive, telling us where to park, asking if we want to go to lunch afterward as a group. A taco stand near the beach?

When I travel for work over the weekend and miss class, I pray for rain back home. I know it is selfish, but if it rains, I am not missing the chance to paint and Laura will reschedule. I do not tell my classmates this—that I hope weather makes it impossible for any of us to paint that day. But they could probably guess. I don't want to miss out, so FOMO (fear of missing out) is the official diagnosis, I suppose.

As soon as I settle in, I sketch onto the canvas in pencil the scene before me, making decisions on how to frame the scene, what to include, distort, or ignore.

Then I paint a wash of turpentine-thinned, light yellow ochre, cadmium red, burnt sienna, chromium oxide green, and cerulean blue—or whatever the scene demands, mixing with titanium white or a touch of black or indigo to get the proper hue.

Next is the work to set down layers. The bold outlines, darker colors first, then I move into sections. Hours pass in the July heat, wearing sunscreen and my straw hat, palette in one hand, paintbrushes and tubes of colors spread beside me in the opened case on the ground.

The brushes I bought in bulk at Blick's that I am using and swapping out frequently are in the pocket of the blue striped XXL man's button-down shirt I use as a painting smock, sable brush tips pointing up. A small tin cup with an ounce or two of turpentine stands ready to clean the brushes between colors; two old rags, cut from bath towels years old, wipe the brushes clean. I usually get paint on my shoes, so I wear the old Reeboks with the holes in the toes.

The genius thing about painting in oils is that it takes so long to dry—days to weeks—that you can simply wipe off the wet paint and start over for a long stretch of time. If only life were so easily reimagined. When I was in my twenties, I painted with acrylics because I thought waiting weeks for an oil painting expression to dry was an impossible ask.

Funny how the less time you have, the more you appreciate and honor the wait.

I am learning to paint in oils, yes, but I am learning to see, focus, pay attention to the smallest details. And I am also learning to revere how buoyant I can feel by finding just the right whiff of blue for a distant wave or how a fine brush can make the difference in expressing movement on a canvas. Oh, and that if you find a particular element too difficult to paint, you can always put a tree in front of it to block the view. I like painting trees.

Joy can start so small and touch everything around me—including me.

I frame the finished paintings that take weeks to dry popped up on a chair in the breakfast room. I wait for a two-for-one sale on frames at Michael's and buy four. I hang the finished works around my house—dozens of them in the family room, living room, dining room, breakfast room, hallways, my bedroom. I give my sons framed paintings or sketches for Christmas—whether or not they want them. I think they genuinely do; there was a conflict over who got the pair of sketches of heads—I think Brendan and Colin worked out a time-share on those.

Even if I am not so satisfied with the outcome—this rock looks like a piece of bread, that flower is shaded improperly, and this person's face is misshapen—there is always an element that I feel I did get magically right and that makes me sincerely proud. The lilies. The sky. The bushes caressing the wall. That leaf, there.

I AM A SIXTY-ONE-YEAR-OLD WHITE SINGLE MOTHER OF THREE grown sons, a woman with privilege, an education, and an identity that has offered me the chance to achieve some professional success. I have lived through a few things—cancer for one, raising three sons alone since they were 6, 4, and 1 after a tumultuous marriage for 10,000 more. They are good men—all working and launched and responsible to the world. Amen.

I also understand what I am not. Because people remind me, sometimes not so kindly.

Looking honestly at a life can be seen as narcissistic navel-gazing, a bald absence of any humility, a waste of time—particularly during and after a pandemic crisis when the world is reshaped. But I do believe I need to take inventory and press the reset button when needed, and I do that through writing; I pretty much always have.

Trying to live with purpose is not simple for me. I am not as gracious, smart, or selfless as Albert Einstein, who professed, "Only the life lived for others is a life worthwhile." I painted that saying in green letters on the wall of the breakfast room in our home twenty-four years ago, hoping it would resonate for my sons, even if for long stretches I was so tired, I did not believe it.

On the same wall above the landline phone no one answers and the cabinets where the place mats and take-out menus are housed, I also painted this quotation from Aristotle: "Happiness depends upon ourselves." I was channeling my father.

While I have written books, taught at a major university, earned some awards for my writing, and mentored thousands of brilliant, smart, and brave thinkers, I am not wildly famous—or rich—from any of it. Even without the trappings of success as a base thermometer, I worry whether what I do and have done is enough for anyone else, let alone for my own aspirations.

In my field as a journalist and author, so many deserving talents—some of them are friends, many are former students, more are my idols—are able through their valiant efforts to uncover truths, change how the world sees and thinks, and influence behaviors and policies shaping ideas in ways I never have and never will. I am simply not as talented or good as they are. They are brave and brilliant and are changing history. I admire them.

I am not envious; I know the capacity I have. Still, I had some audacious dreams and ambitions for myself; upon reflection now, I see them as dreams that I will never fulfill. Of course now and forever there is a world full of innovators who are better than me at anything and everything. Obvious, yes, and as time runs short, confronting.

Even when modified for age, I am not anyone's ideal for beauty, never have been, though I know I am blessed and I also know the curse that appearance matters. I agree that the particular framing of appearance is always unfairly twisted in favor of white American youth, brimming with stereotypes and ableism, with little room for nuance let alone difference or nonconformity to an antiquated, forced, unattainable concrete mold. Jia Tolentino wrote about it in the *New Yorker*, calling the popular measure of beauty the "Instagram Face—it was as if the algorithmic tendency to flatten everything into a composite of greatest hits had resulted in a beauty ideal that favored white women capable of manufacturing a look of rootless exoticism."

Life and an accumulation of unplanned events happened to my mind and to my body. It shows.

Watching awards shows—the Kennedy Center Honors come to mind—I see the musicians, actors, and stunning performers just a wee bit older than me celebrated for years and years and years of breathtaking excellence and genius. I applaud and marvel at their achievements, but my second thought is, "I'll never be great at anything." That my appreciation of mastery bounces back to me is also a character flaw. I know.

Though I believe I make the perfect bruschetta with asiago cheese bread sliced thin or occasionally write a compelling sentence, I am mediocre or worse at most things I try and have done—even if I have tried those things the requisite thousands of times that you must do something until you can call yourself an expert. I expected I would do more, be more, give more.

My indulgent intention in this collection of essays is in understanding who I am and why—particularly at this third act of my life and career when there is more behind than ahead. Millions of us are doing the same; I know because I meet you at conferences and parties and on the train, in waiting rooms and airports. We are telling each other our stories, listening to how we are more alike than not. I want to connect with these stories at a confusing and confronting time personally and culturally when the world as we knew it is disrupted, transformed, upended and in many cases eradicated as a result of COVID-19. In the shadows of concurrent race-related tragedies and calls for action, interrogating a life like mine can seem either ridiculous or reasonable.

How can I make the best of it all? Am I ever enough?

I recently interviewed Co-CEO of LifeLabs Learning Tania Luna, a Ukraine refugee whose TED Talk in New York yielded 1.8 million views. I was profiling her for a business blog I write. Tania told me that everyone needs a pause. It can be a micro-pause or a macropause, but you can't always be on overdrive. Ambition is a virtue, but exhaustion is not. You become reactive and defensive if you fail to step back, stop, think, consider your options, consider others. Frenzy is a barrier to purpose.

"The biggest problem most of us get into is a lot of times we know the right thing to do but we don't ask ourselves, why am I doing this?" Tania told me. "So before you delegate or get defensive, it's good to develop a pausing habit."

Most women my age whom I know personally and professionally are not able to pause so much; working hard and facing health challenges, heartbreaks, financial setbacks, illnesses or deaths of partners, parents, friends, and children. Some have a spouse whose health is catastrophic, placing them into daily caregiving again. In spite of all that, they are also at times deliriously happy.

I interviewed author Mary Pipher for a story recently; she had just written a book, *Women Rowing North: Navigating Life's Currents and Flourishing as We Age*. Ten years my senior, she was breaking down for me a road map both on and off the record. "Happiness depends on how we deal with what we are given," she said.

Like most women I know, I am trying to see clearly, craft, decode, and reshape an identity as a mature woman, single or partnered, with or without grandchildren, with or without a secure financial future. I am new to being old; at times it feels like I am wearing someone else's clothes in the wrong size. All of this self-doubt and insecurity does not erase my gratitude. It clouds it. My gratitude often peeks through those clouds.

This elective self-exam erupts at an extremely stressful and confusing political stretch of history where you can't rely on truth as an absolute, when gaslighting in the public sphere is as relentless and persistent as a recurring volcanic eruption or series of earthquakes.

It feels—and is—unsafe in many spaces for so many people; percolating rage for injustices named and dutifully called out based on gender, race, age, ability, geography, ideology, orientation, religion, socioeconomics. A torrent of hardships borne from the global pandemic created physical, economic, emotional, and social scars that may never heal. It is not just wearisome to read the news and unmask what is fact and what are lies, but it feels like a threat to every breath. In that arena, deciding whether and how I matter at all and how I can inform one small piece of the world is another challenge to take on when every second absorbing public realities is disruptive, disturbing, and disorienting. It also feels like it could be a waste of time when there is so much real injustice to unravel and remedy.

I get it that there is no guarantee for anyone ever for what, how, and when life happens, but I am shaken—and shaking—with the notion that the finish line is just ahead and I'd better get moving, get more stuff done; it's lights out soon enough. I'd better create my impact and accomplish whatever I can while I can. I will never be good enough. I seek forgiveness for myself for not meeting my own expectations.

Yes, I am lucky because at this point, due to my privilege and circumstance, I get to choose deliberate and intentional paths. I am no longer daily caretaking: both my parents have passed, my sons are raised. Many of my habits have cemented—I am not going to give up French onion dip, coloring my hair, or working hard—but I have given up diet soda.

And while I get it that this life is not all about me, I do want to ask the questions about just why, how, or if anything I do affects anyone or anything. Do I matter?

"Get over yourself," I say to myself in the mirror, then go on brushing my teeth, followed by the gum care whitening mouthwash, because why not, and skip the floss even though I hear it would add years to my life.

I understand that a key factor in arriving at clarity comes from examining truths, encounters, and the magic as well as the mess of the past, an apologetic nod to all blind spots, amnesia, bias, intentional and unintentional shifting and stretching of mutable memories.

All to say if this is to be my Lifetime movie–worthy self-discovery journey that middle-aged and older women seem to need, it will all have to take place close to home a few hours a week because I work a lot. I also don't have the time and money to explore who I am solo abroad. I can't summer in Tuscany; eat, pray, and love across the globe; or even walk 1,000 miles through deserts and national parks to find answers. I have bills and deadlines. I would overpack.

I am finding clarity by writing this book. The wish is that this journey may parallel yours and in this space you may also see yourself or someone you love, and it may be helpful. A little.

I understand that my parents approached most all of their questions about life, identity, and purpose through their impenetrable faith, assuming that grace will always arrive. And I guess that was what both my mother and father were saying, when they told us to act like we're having a good time, to go into any situation positively, be happy with who and where you are. And grace will arrive. Often it does.

✴ PART ONE ✴

LIFE

ROOTS

EVERY SPRING I PLANT BEGONIAS OR IMPATIENS AROUND MY favorite tree's base. I learned not to plant the white impatiens because from half a block away, they look like wadded toilet paper. This year I planted purple, pink, and coral impatiens. If it rains enough and I water long enough on dry days, they broaden their reach, hold hands, and encircle the tree like a gemstone bracelet.

The tree must be eighty feet tall. When I stand on my front porch, squint at the beloved elm tree in the front yard, and pinch my thumb and forefinger into brackets, I can measure just the right amount for ten feet, then stack eight of those on top of each other. I understand squinting and pinching are not truly precise.

For the past few years Dutch elm disease has been claiming many trees on this block, in this neighborhood, like a fever. The process is the same: one morning the white trucks with the flashing yellow lights arrive, the hard-hatted, orange-vested workers cluster near the tree talking loudly over the humming of the saws. One of them alights in a white-bucketed cherry picker, the outstretched limbs of the tree fastened to rope so they fall where planned with a thud on the ground you can hear from across the street. Only two or more hours later, the tree is gone and the trunk divided into neat, full thick spirals the size of small tables piled on the lawn.

My tree—I call it my tree, though it does not belong to me as it is on the public parkway—has been spared.

More than twenty-four years I've lived in this house, this complicated old friend of a house, more like a second cousin, a witness to the emotional intimacy of a family. It is where the imperfections and distrust of a family were ground into saw-dust, sprinkled with the reassurance of recurring joy of a family that would not be broken, even if bent. It is where visible and invisible affection was a safety net.

I plan to leave this house, this marvelous, magnificent house I am often too tired and too distracted to maintain as it needs and deserves. This house I am so lucky to have owned, thanks to my brother Paul and my late mother.

It is time. Nothing dramatic has happened, everything dramatic has happened. This house full of laughter and love. This house full of sobbing and shouting and indelible hurt. This place where my three sons and I became who we are as a family. This place where it was known who we are not. This place that holds in its red bricks and plaster the disappointments and the smiles. This address that sheltered us with security and warmth, that held no secrets, though many times I wish it had. It is where the secrets were told, spilled, shouted. Some of us should have been spared the disclosure. It is where trust scaffolded our daily lives.

Until recently, I lived alone—most of it in this big house—for a total of nine months over thirty-one years. Married, then not, mother to one, two, three. My time alone over three decades was the stint when my middle son and my youngest son were both away at college from August 2012 to May 2013—different

4

colleges with different tuition amounts but the same due date for the enormous bills.

In that stretch of singularity I sometimes ate Triscuits for dinner standing up without dirtying a plate or a fork. One load of laundry a week, maybe every two weeks. A friend suggested I just take my underwear and rinse it out in the shower when needed and skip the whole washing machine–dryer cycles of laundry all together. Hand wash whatever. Or not at all. I wonder: how long could I go without ever turning on the washer?

Each of my sons moved back home at some point after graduating college, a domino effect of boomeranging; one has been gone a year or so, one was back six months, another stayed for a while and is now moved out. I love them, of course, and they are welcome. I am fortunate I can help, and this is their home. But I also like being alone—acknowledging that there is a difference between elective independence and mandated quarantine. I like being alone like I was in the '80s on Wrightwood Avenue in the studio apartment with DeAnne down the hall, a quick walk to the 151 bus. I was alone on Cedar Street, seventeenth floor. I crave the reliability when you have no one to rely on but yourself. I am reliable.

In all those years I have done what I was supposed to do. Without uttered rebellion, without fail, as the mother of these three humans, the sole custodial parent, as the keeper of this house, as the glue for this family. Write the bills for the mortgage, the insurance, the tuition, Verizon, AT&T, Commonwealth Edison, Nicor Gas. Snow removal. Lawn maintenance. File cabinets full of paid bills and receipts. The parking tickets I did not earn, the missed tolls with the penalties.

The refrigerator is empty, the refrigerator is full. Raspberries, cauliflower, milk, sliced turkey at $7.99 a pound. Parmesan, eggs, coffee creamer; did you know the sugar-free creamer has fewer calories than the low-fat? So many cereal boxes—all of them opened and none of them with the wax paper closed tightly.

Nothing has time to spoil; nothing perhaps except me.

Refill, refresh, recharge, all to maintain my role as director of procurement. Update the supplies. Replenish. An assembly line of products and produce and fuel. Not what I said or felt was necessary, it seemed, but the refilling was. Constant motion to fill up the people in my charge, the children I love. And like every parent working, I am to simultaneously fill up my résumé and pretend everything is fine when I drive away from this house and walk onto a stage, into a classroom, or press *send* on a manuscript. A life partitioned into cubicles of need for work or family, forfeiting the option to create and maintain a cubicle of my own.

I know it is arrogant to complain, to express my bald dissatisfaction with a lucky, blessed life. But it is a dissatisfaction women, parents, and mothers like me rarely utter aloud. Or type. Yes, I could afford to replenish. I could mostly afford to pay the bills, keep the job, sign the new contract, deposit payments in my bank account. If I couldn't afford it, I took on more contract work, hoping or knowing the next month would be better. I have held more than one job at once since graduating college. I consistently signed on for one full-time job and a sprinkling of other regular work not just to earn more and make ends meet for a family of four, but to be more, to try to catapult my career forward. To matter.

Mostly my life moved forward because I worked hard and stayed quiet when a boss was unkind or unfair. Kept mum when I felt disparities sent my way because that is what you do when you are the breadwinner. Like millions of others, I never had the luxury of quitting. You do the work to pay for the bread—and the Gatorade. Because it is your house and your family. And you are it.

Yet it is impossible not to feel empty when you are emptied every day.

WHEN HURRICANE HARVEY BLIGHTED TEXAS IN THE SUMMER of 2017, I saw hundreds of Twitter photographs and videos on

Google news of flood-choked homes, streets, buildings, and highways. The wading, desperate rescue scenes, the pets in cages carried in boats, shock-eyed and damp, surprised at their fate.

One photograph that humbled me was one so many people might remember of the eight older women residents of La Vita Bella, an assisted living home in Dickinson, Texas. The women, in their seventies and eighties, or so it seems, are seated in faux leather recliner chairs, some in wheelchairs, their faces calm and expressionless, as someone said, as if it were photoshopped. In the photo, the women are dry from the chest up, but their torsos and legs are immersed in the gray, thick water that fills what must be the main living area, with a red popcorn machine in the corner, wet and ruined. A half-dozen plastic bottles of clean water sit on a table, taunting in their irony. Funny, I thought, they live in a place with a name that means "the beautiful life" in the feminine form of the noun. Soaking and trapped in the water, they sat there for ten hours until they were rescued by the National Guard.

A few days later, a photo of the same women shows them mostly smiling and happy, seven older women in fresh, dry clothes, seated in front of a grand piano, their blue-socked feet curled. This is the after photo, proving they have survived it all. They were patient. There was a happy after.

We had a flood in our house—two actually—but none ever as bad as Harvey or Irma, which arrived days later in Florida. Nothing as horrific as Hurricane Maria in Puerto Rico; the recovery is still in progress in 2020 and may never be complete.

I understand from the stance of privilege that flooding caused by a river is an inconvenience and not the magnitude of a hurricane or tornado that wipes out families and everything they own; when people die, without access to healthcare, life-saving medicines, dialysis, treatments. It is not equivalent; my experience is superficial and minor. I could afford to call service companies, to have help, to file insurance claims. We were never in physical danger.

The first flood from the swollen Des Plaines River in 2009 brought three feet of sewer water filling the basement, the man cave, where Brendan had his bedroom. Black water everywhere. Webs of shiny black globs clinging to the walls.

It had been a rainstorm of more than seven inches of rain in a few hours that resulted in one of the worst floods in Chicago's history that July night. A swift flow of water from a backed-up sewer rushed in from a back basement door, filling every inch of the area where my sons often played video games and their friends slept over. Neighbors up and down the block were all dealing with the same issues. We were all soaked; some neighbors on Clinton Avenue had water as high as four feet. On William Street, I heard later, the water rose to the ceilings of some basements.

On the finished, carpeted side of our basement were the bookshelves and Brendan's bed, dressers, and clothes. On the other side of the stairs was the laundry and storage area, plus the treadmill that I vowed to use more often than I did. It was destroyed.

Drenched and dripping were hundreds of my newspaper clippings from the 1980s pulled from metal file cabinets. Wet was the fake Christmas tree—crammed into a plastic bin turned sideways, its thin opening at the seal quickly filling with water so that inside my favorite burgundy and forest green velvet tree skirt was also ruined. Brendan's box spring and mattress were soaked through, plus the seats of two other couches, Weldon's twin-size mattress and box spring from college, three end tables, lamps, bookcases, and the built-in wood bar, original to the house constructed in 1934.

The following morning, the flood damage cleaning service arrived with a crew of six. Before noon, two men had sawed my late mother's yellow floral couch in half. It was the couch that reminded me so much of her, with its butterfly pattern; the one in her den on Ashland Avenue, the house where she last lived. It had mahogany claw-and-ball feet, a sturdy back, broad arms, and a full shape. It was significantly nicer than the rest of the furniture in my basement, like the sleeper couch with the turquoise and mauve Southwestern print that I bought for guests in 1988 after Weldon was born and the guest room became his nursery.

The constant whirrrr of the chain saw—like the sounds of cutting down a tree—the smell of the musty wood, damp and fetid, the hustling blur of workers filling shiny black contractor bags with tiles, paneling, baseboards, carpet, shelving, all of it a full-on endorsement that so much needed to go. The men carried the pieces of my mother's couch leaking its thick, beige stuffing, coils exposed, to the curb in front of my house. There they heaped it all onto a pile that eventually grew to 30 feet wide and 10 feet high before it was hauled away. They stripped the floor to the concrete base and pried the paneling from the walls.

Within eight weeks and the help of insurance, a contractor succeeded in putting the basement back together, this time with vinyl tile floors and DuraRock walls. All the clutter was gone. Brendan's closet had a new vinyl door, and in the alcove where the built-in bar had been, I put his new bed I bought from Al on North Avenue who owns a shop called Al-Mart that I frequent not just for the discounts and the free delivery but because there really is an Al. Across from Brendan's new bed, I placed a borrowed sofa, armoire, rugs, and anything else I could scrap together from family and friends. I would be scavenging yard sales for whatever else I needed. Another chance to start anew.

A friend who heard the news of our flood dropped off a bottle of wine and a box of chocolates with a card that read, "My barn's burnt down, now I can see the sky."

MORE TIME PASSES, SEASONS BLOOM AND FALL, THIS HOUSE rides in and out each year with a new affliction—inside and out. The couches need to be cleaned, the wood floors tended, a storm window breaks, the air conditioner in the family room stops working. The ceiling in one bedroom has bubbles. The slate roof loses shingles from a hailstorm.

The furniture on the back porch did not last as long as I had hoped, as long as was promised. Maybe those pieces should never have lasted this long—fifteen years—their green plastic meshing unraveling on the arms, the backs, the seats. I have repainted the arms with white enamel spray paint. I have missed some rusting spots. How spoiled I am to complain, that this house I own needs attention. I can pay to keep it. I can pay to heat and cool it, though my favorite months of the year are the "free months" of April to June and September to mid-November without air-conditioning or heat, just opening and shutting the windows. I know I am lucky. I am only tired. I work to keep the house together like I work to keep my family together.

I paid to have fixed the crumbling wall on the north side of the basement, the garage that is leaning, the back porch that needed new stairs. The list of what more is to fix is too long to arrange or pay for at once. I have a contractor who lets me pay in installments. He recently sealed the outside brick wall facing south, told me it would hold for a handful of years more.

So many years in this house of frenzied dissonance. So many birthday parties, graduations, Thanksgiving dinners with the cornbread stuffing, brussels sprouts with olive oil and balsamic, and the pecan pie from the Wolfgang Puck cookbook, its pages stained with brown sugar, water, and butter. Love and loyalty in its foundation.

When my sons and I arrived at this house in 1996, I was months past a divorce. We moved to the house my brother Paul had owned and cared for so painstakingly as he was moving to another house. All three of my boys were small and kinetic. The first thing we needed was a gate off the driveway to the backyard. I did not want them to get hurt, run in the street. They needed to be contained. I needed to contain my family and be safe.

I will not miss the property taxes that made so much sense when the boys were all in local grade school, middle school, high school—the good schools with the high test scores and the teachers who stay after hours long after they need to. I won't miss the blue-and-gold striped awnings—though they do keep out the summer heat—that go up and down every year, with a hanging and takedown invoice each time as well as storage costs.

We grew roots here. Two decades of the flotsam and jetsam of their lives inhabit nearly every corner. The narrow closets filled with clothes worn too often or never at all, the cabinets filled with important papers—how important are the papers, who decides?

"Don't give away any of my clothes," Colin declared at six years old.

Why?

"Because when I am famous, they will be worth a lot."

"Even the Power Ranger pajamas?" I ask.

Shoes in the mudroom, so many, when do they wear them? So many running shoes. Mud crusted in the grooves of the soles. Flip-flops, swim shoes. The time we went to Miami and everyone needed them because the beach was covered in shells that hurt our feet. I put the hotel room charges on Visa.

Fancy plates in the breakfront of the dining room bursting with wedding gifts of silver that need to be polished, a wedding for a marriage that didn't last as long as the presents. My mother's yellow plates, that citrus yellow that makes you thirsty and long for crisp vegetables and moist fruit. My grandmother's plates with the flowers around the edges like a painting; they are more than one hundred years old. Teacups, saucers. Sugar bowls. Gravy boats. I can count how many times I used them.

Why was I not more fervent, more Marie Kondo, more militant about feng shui and minimalism and throwing away something every time I came into the house with something new. I know why I did not throw anything away. Because I was afraid I could not replace. No, I knew I could not replace. Keep the chair,

I will glue on the leg. I cannot buy another chair. Let me fix the broken whatever, the broken anything, the broken me, and someday, sometime I will have time and money to fix it.

But do not throw it away. I was afraid of throwing away any part of the boys' lives. But it is too much. There are decades of history here for four people. I am the curator of every piece of lint.

I will eventually move out of this house after I clean out and repaint the three bathroom cabinets filled with the prescriptions from the '00s on their shelves—you never know—and I will fill with plaster the tennis ball–sized hole in the wall behind my bed made by a plumber who swore that was how you fixed the drain in the bathtub and then just left it there, without filling it back in or taping it or anything. I will fix the closet doors that the boys slammed or punched or threw themselves against, find a knob for the door to the third bedroom upstairs.

Likely I will need to replace the dishwasher. God knows I have to fix the garbage disposal. I asked Colin to disconnect and remove the off switch because after ten or so years if you turned it on, it would not turn off. That permanent "on" arrived after several months of mysteriously and intermittently turning itself on. I could be upstairs, asleep and the three boys in their beds, silent in their rooms, and the disposal would turn on with an angry growl. The first time I jumped up and imagined someone was mowing the lawn in the dining room, but quickly figured it out. No one else woke up.

All these photos framed on every surface. The baptisms, the first Communions, the confirmations—any and all of the sacraments. Brendan receiving his university diploma. Weldon, Colin too. And the weddings of friends and family where I am smiling, sometimes happy, sometimes just going through the motions. The staged photos by the fireplace that took maybe fifteen shots to get right. The family parties, the vacations when they were little and when I sometimes wished there was another adult to at least help carry the bags.

Here is this life. Here is where we spent the afternoons, the mornings, the late nights. We shared the dinners of favorite meals around the breakfast room table with the green chairs; I wiped the marinara sauce off the floor, the splatters of oil off the wall near the stove. The times we were all in sync, caught on the same high-wire act and even if it is just for a split second, when you all see the same view and it is glorious.

The times when unspeakably cruel things were said, some denied, most assumed forgotten. The broken promises, the shattered expectations. But sometimes, many sometimes, for a nanosecond you collide in the same messy and delicious memory. Before each one splits into his own version of the Snapchat shot and it is never the same view again at all.

The laughter. Sometimes I hear the laughter in my head—Brendan's imitations, Weldon's jokes, Colin's guffaw that is loud and infectious.

It is going to take a long time to get to the bones of this house and to remove all that we have done to it—to neutralize the space, remove the evidence of all that has transpired. My friend Sue says when she moved out of the big house she had with her two children and by herself into a swanky condo with a view, she got a Dumpster and just starting hurling into it relics of the past. She says she kept some things but threw away photo albums and all her Christmas decorations. She even threw away some framed photographs of her children, merciless in her pruning to the basics. No one was traumatized.

I understand how I am manufactured; I acknowledge how I am built with full-on inhabitance of emotion that grants me at times a sadness so life-sized it gives me hives and a throat-tightening despair when I am hurt. Or afraid. I also see how a small gesture can shift to rapture, over a butterfly on the back steps or a text from Weldon with a GIF that makes me laugh out loud. I know how I connect to the places that define me. This place defines me. It defines us. It exists because and in spite of me, and it exists for my sons. They had a home, a solid house they could come to, they still come to, and where they can stay. We belonged here.

OUR CHILDREN—AMONG OTHER ROLES—SERVE THE DELIGHTFUL purpose of keeping us connected to the passage of time. The milestones somersault over each other, some predictably, others off course, but always there nonetheless. They show you that you are not standing still, that you mark time in terms of how you affect the other people you touch and care for and how it relates to their movement forward and away.

For years, decades—a lifetime—you can proceed this way, checking off the boxes of their development, and then the tasks it took to get them there at each stage start to bleed and leak over each other, one not ending before a tangential task begins. The months, the years of trials, complications, challenges, worries— will it end up OK? One mistake promoting a do-over or a recount or an erasure. So much that it never seems neat and you lose sight of the shore and realize you are rowing in circles with no compass. Lost.

In my imagination the befores and afters that have accumu- lated in my kaleidoscope life seem so simple and exact, a defining moment as clear as a road stripe, yellow paint on smooth, black tar. First she was married, then she was not. First she was young, then she was not. First she raised her children, then they were grown. First it was all possible, then it was not. First there were dreams, then there were none.

Separating the compartments of yourself this way makes it appear more definitive than any of it is; less of a murky soup and more of a bento box of events, walled off distinctly and neatly. Predictable. It is the cosmic joke saved for the myopic to believe that circumstance will not annihilate the rules and that logic will win; that plans are heeded, that the walls in the box are left standing.

As time moves like a steady, unrelenting wind through the

house, the marks of accomplishments and events would be as clear as the pencil marks on the walls and doorways in the homes of parents who would allow their children to write on the walls. Not me. In those other people's homes, these marks show you are not standing still; you mark your time in terms of how you affect the other people you care for. It is about their progress, their growth, their movement away. Some of us do not need the permanent marker reminders. Our hearts are marked.

IN HOTEL ROOMS WHERE I TOUCH DOWN FOR A WORK TRIP, I greedily watch reality shows about losing hundreds and hundreds of pounds, traveling across the globe to see the ninety-day fiancé, preparing an elaborate cake in the shape of cartoon characters for an event for one thousand, tearing down houses to rebuild mansions. I even like the shows about choosing the perfect wedding dress, and I marvel that the women in the episodes complain about the bodice but never the price. In those shows, the befores and afters seem so simple and exact, a defining moment. Before and after the commercial, the big reveal.

That is the part I feel most misinformed by; that I believed there was a before and after my children were grown; with mountains of time for myself and a view of the lake from a balcony above the twelfth-floor condo where I imagine that I live deliriously happy. I look at ads for one- and two-bedroom condos longingly, woozy with possibility, a driving thirst for clean lines and floor-to-ceiling windows, a canopy bed and thick peach silk curtains, lined and puddled on the floor.

In my dream of the future, for some reason I am taller. I am prettier and happier in my after, fewer lines on my face; I have firmer arms. I feel settled. I do not need so much Tylenol. I do not need a haircut desperately, and my feet are polished, the bottoms smoothed and cared for, not rough and flaking, testimonials to my barefoot strolls outside. My house smells like the expensive candles from Anthropologie, not the poor imitations I buy at Marshall's on sale for $6.99. I would not feel this disquiet, so incomplete, like a discard in the clearance bin at Target.

I would have more time off work in the after I dreamed of, not so many weekly conference calls on Zoom where some people eat lunch on screen; not so many Uber rides to the airport; not so many invoices that take hours to create; not so many emails, not so much feedback that is sometimes impatient; not so many conversations about deadlines, meetings, clients, stories, things that need to be done, replaced, edited, created, fixed. Not so much proving myself, worrying about "personalities" and the feelings of the people who mind deeply when I answer an email with a simple "yup." There would be no manufactured drama. It would just be work and we would be kind to each other, patting each other on the back, toasting success. Happy.

In my fantasy, I imagine the contents of our basement magically disappeared, skipping the storage. Having saved the photo albums and the trophies and the art projects and the things I just could not throw away, I would take photos of the items, finally give up and toss. No one would miss them or complain. Though I would like to keep the storage bin with all the beach towels and the wonderful beach mat my sister Madeleine gave me that is straw (or maybe it is bamboo) and you can roll it and tie it together to carry, the size of an encyclopedia.

I will always keep the earrings from my mother, the cross my father wore in World War II , the fuchsia silk couches, these monuments to them that hold my memories intact, fuse them upright like Corinthian columns. I have several of my father's watches and clocks, and none of them work.

I picture myself in my next life with a new queen-size bed, not the one that I sleep in now that is from the 1980s. In my dream, it's a new bed, with a new mattress—the pillow-top kind—new sheets, not the ones I have slept in for years and wash each week in a weekend flurry of tidiness. I picture the second bedroom as a tidy office with no one's worn damp black socks on the center coffee table or on my writing desk. No dirty dishes and half-empty cups marking the table space in rings and crumbs.

Like a lot of people, I've never had a kitchen like the ones featured in the magazines with the steel appliances and the dishwasher with as many settings as in the cockpit of a small airplane. I've never had a floor I didn't need to sweep twice a day because the dirt shows. I've never had a quiet dishwasher; those make me suspicious. I know none of what I've lived through is hardship or difficult. Or even inconvenient.

Years ago when I was a single working mother gasping in panic with the boys young and in school, I fantasized about what it would be like not to have to hire someone to watch the boys so I could walk out the door to work. That phase has been over for ten years, but what did I see for myself when I was this age I am now? Another place, another me. I did not know I would still sometimes cry at night and in the shower. That I would have real longing. And regret.

EVERY JULY I CALL THE SAME PLUMBING COMPANY TO SCHEDULE someone to come out and clear my drains and pipes, from the backyard to the front yard and out to the sewer. They are nice there, everyone from Robert whose last name is on the truck to the woman who takes your number and someone calls right back. They have a female plumber: she is in her twenties; she is nice. One of the young men who comes out on a call to fix a toilet or a sink knows my son Colin, and wrestled at the high school, as all my boys did. The plumbing team is polite and prompt and sometimes bills me instead of demanding a check right then and there. If they come in the house, they put on paper booties to save my rugs. I guess some customers want that.

What they do every July is called "root incursion" because the tree roots enter the pipes and basically clog it all up. This can be expensive if you let it go too long, and you might have to replace all the sewer pipes—and let me tell you, that is neither cheap nor pretty. It's best to just keep your roots under control. Edit them. The big tree in the front of the house is the biggest culprit.

I admit I have not edited my roots.

Our roots grew here in this house, this redbrick Colonial I was blessed to live in at all. We each put down our roots and they grew. Thick, gnarling roots groping, plunging into each other's tender dirt, mud, and clay. The rainwater helped them spread. Sometimes too much. Sometimes it flooded.

My oldest son, Weldon, has a tattoo on his right shoulder of a tree with colored leaves and flowers, the size of a large grapefruit. He got it a few years back. It is a fairy-tale tree, more Grimm than Seuss, with a firm, thick brown trunk and four strong branches, each winding boldly across his flesh with scores of full green leaves. The base is supported with roots that are thinner, but symmetrical and even, closely connected.

I asked him if it hurt.

THE ELECTRIC FRYING PAN

"C'EST FROMAGE!"

The uniformed valet who resembled an extra in a 1930s Myrna Loy movie had carelessly piled our blue cooler atop some of our eight suitcases that he was commandeering in the lobby as my father checked us into the hotel.

Really, it was his fault—the valet's, I mean. I know he was probably more used to Louis Vuitton bags—the fancy leather suitcases with the printed initials, metal locks, and handles that he could maneuver two, maybe three at a time. I doubt he had ever handled so many vinyl suitcases for one reservation plus an American cooler filled with the likes of what my mother had packed for the eight of us. The hungry eight of us.

I didn't know much French, just the basic *le chien* (the dog) and *mon dieu* (OMG, in today's parlance) to satisfy a first-grade nun and make it seem as though I deserved the Gallic origins of my name. I just knew it was about the plastic container of cottage cheese (indeed, as I would later learn, "That's cheese!" is what the valet exclaimed) that had just tumbled out of the blue cooler and spilled a white lumpy liquid mess on the lobby floor. Along with the pound of Oscar Mayer bacon. And the bag of ice, half melted and also leaking onto the marble foyer.

My father had just checked us into Le Chateau Frontenac in Quebec, this 1965 summer, and we were quietly and dutifully preparing to proceed to our set of three adjoining rooms like a line of girls in the Madeline books I loved and was convinced were named after my sister Madeleine even if they spelled her name wrong. Obedient procession in public places was our routine; my older sisters Mary Pat, Maureen, and Madeleine marching into one room. My brothers Bill and Paul in another, and me, age seven , on a cot in a room with my mom and dad. I loved it when my mother allowed me to unlock the secret connecting doors.

As if I were in charge of the secrets.

Now following quietly like she taught us, the six of us trailed behind our mother in the iridescent lobby. The couches, the curtains, the chandeliers, it all resembled a scene out of *Mary Poppins* or *The Sound of Music*, not the outdoor scenes, but the indoor ones; I didn't know where to look first. My father always stayed behind dawdling at the registration desk. Sometimes I thought it was to be sure everything would be just right, but now I think it might have been to stay back and pretend for just a few moments anyway that he was some debonair bachelor all by himself taking his time to linger at the hotel desk, not the father of six whose wife has read all the guidebooks and mailed in a reservation request, receiving a brochure in return.

This is how dreams are made, I thought: you make them happen by mailing away for them.

Months in advance, my mother went to the library and checked out the guidebooks on any city she wanted us to visit and mailed away for a reservation—for hotels, restaurants, museums, Broadway shows if the trip was to New York. She would research what to do and where to go. Dreams come true at the price of a stamp, I thought. I didn't have any concept of payment, money, or cost. I used to think the factory my father ran was an actual mint that printed money, the way that my mother said, "Dad needs to make money," and the way that he sometimes responded that he had to make more money whenever we asked for extra things or my mother talked about painting a room in the house.

As the moneymaker, my father (as I pictured it) worked every day with sleeves rolled up running dollar bills through a printing press or cutting coins with an enormous machine. I knew his company was a manufacturing plant that made starter drives for cars, trucks, and boats, but I also believed he printed money. At sixteen, I worked for him in his office in the plant on Division Street and Cicero Avenue doing the filing of bills and invoices. I loved seeing him at his desk with all the pictures of us on the bookshelves. By then I had figured out that the factory was not also a mint.

Like everything my mother did, the Canada trip this year was meticulously prepared, starting with the flip-books she mailed away for months in advance from the American Automobile Association, Triple A. The maps showed the route in green marker, and I could thumb through the pages, bored and impatient, sitting between my parents in the front seat of the wood-paneled Chrysler station wagon. She had all the details in place, including everything we put into each of our suitcases, all tucked tight without any wiggle room onto the roof's steel rack. We had to make a list of what we would pack, she would check to make sure we had good clothes for church—we went to Mass on vacations—and underwear. Once I forgot to pack underwear and we had to make an unplanned stop because Madeleine, Mary, and Maureen were older than me and theirs wouldn't fit. The night before every family trip, my father was in the garage or in the driveway with a diagram of the positioning of all eight suitcases, so they would fit on the luggage rack and he could tie them down. Secure.

In the lobby, my mother looked the part of the loving matron, always wearing a suit—one of her ribbon suits or tweed skirt and matching jacket with pearls, good shoes, stockings. She would have hated how most people travel today—yoga pants, flip-flops, sweatshirts, for goodness sake! Hair unkempt! Pajamas out in public! Mom got her hair "done" for these big occasions, even if when she came back from the beauty parlor, as she called it, you couldn't touch her hair and bend it because it was super-stiff, as if they sprayed a whole can of Aquanet on her head. She despised the leisure suits of the '70s, said everyone looked ridiculous in their bright-colored pseudopajamas; comfort was not a virtue she would declare. My father always wore a tie when we flew in airplanes, and a jacket—I think so he could tuck the eight plane tickets into the inside of his coat.

We were all dressed up too, my two brothers in khaki pants and good shoes, button-down shirts, vests and sweaters if it was chilly. My sisters and I? The four of us in dresses or skirts, we didn't match each other most of the time, that was just once in a while, like the royal blue velvet dresses with the lace collars for Christmas or the black velvet skirts and vests my mother made for us, the ones with the gold braided trim that I thought were spectacular. Cher had nothing on me except that she was a foot or two taller and had that long, raven hair and those bright white teeth. And a husband who really couldn't sing.

I learned a lot from my mother, not just about going to special places but how organized your home can be. What I didn't know was that my mother was not like most other mothers—not until I started to have sleepovers and afternoons to play (that was before they called them "play dates"). Friends from school or on the block would just call up on the phone or walk over to your backyard and call out, "Want to come over?" And we would walk there.

But I wasn't prepared for when you go to other people's houses and see socks strewn on the stairs—when company is over! You start to feel special and a little bit bad that maybe you are spoiled like your brothers sometimes say you are, and that maybe your mother is different and not just because she takes you to the opera and the Goodman Theatre and tells you that you can be whatever you want to be and never once laughs when you say you will be an author and you will be famous.

My mother was one part Auntie Mame with a splash of Jackie Kennedy—smelled good too, like Chanel No. 5 (though I had never heard of 1 through 4)—but she was also extremely practical, frugal even. Every vacation we took, she brought a cooler of food for the road for snacks and drinks, and replenished it before check-in so we had food for her to make breakfast in the room. No cereal for this crowd, and cereal bars had not been invented, though there were those chewy Space Food Sticks, but those didn't count for a meal.

I swore that when I grew up, I would be daring and carefree and not plan every meal ahead of time, especially not breakfast. I would stop along the road, casually, willy-nilly, spur of the moment, see what restaurant suited my taste at that particular second, be spontaneous. Fried chicken? Why, yes—no, no, wait, hamburgers, no, let's try beef sandwiches, or maybe just ice cream. Ice cream it is. Snap of the fingers, none of this premeditated tedium. And I would never travel with a cooler. I would be a jet-setter—that's right, have a purse on one arm, a small bag in the other, and not a hint of preparation afforded for my next meal. You never saw Marilyn Monroe or Angie Dickinson toting a cooler. Or Catherine Deneuve.

There it was, the cooler on the lobby floor, the cottage cheese in a murky splash, and the valet having a cow, as my sister Maureen would always say. But my mother ignored the shock and indignation of the valet and the looks of the patrons in the lobby, picking up the Oscar Meyer bacon like it was the most natural thing in the world, all in one elegant swoop, grabbing the cooler with the other hand, her bucket purse pushed higher on her forearm. She left the cottage cheese, put the other contents back into the cooler, shut it tight, placed it back on the pile, and continued to the elevators. She was the model of impunity, immune to embarrassment, acting as if it was all the valet's fault, which it was. He was immobile, his mouth still agape. Someone from behind the desk came out to clean it up. We knew not to speak, not to gesture, not to draw attention to ourselves like she pinched us not to do in church, which I thought was some kind of sin, my mother said it so much.

My father was by now acting as if he was not in any way related to any of us. This is when he started his nervous coughing.

My mother proceeded to the elevator and the valet rushed to catch up, the six of us folded into the elevator now cramped with the luggage rack, and just before the door closed, my father entered. My mother was not angry, still had not acknowledged verbally the cottage cheese that was most assuredly against some hotel rule, like when you can't bring your own snacks into the movie theater (there was even a sign that told you not to). But yes, we did that too. We all sat through *Doctor Zhivago* at the Lake Theater in Oak Park with plastic baggies of homemade popcorn, Jiffy Pop you made on the stove. This was before microwaves, when if you didn't have Jiffy Pop, you heated the oil in the pan and shook the kernels around lying there in a mottled oily mass of brown and beige and then put the top on real quick or the fluffy poofs would fly across the stove and land on the kitchen floor.

Once the suitcases were sorted out and everyone headed to their shared rooms, we laughed about the cottage cheese and the look on the valet's face, as if a head had rolled out or a finger, some ghastly body part that meant we were criminals or murderers, not just a family with some bacon and cottage cheese in a cooler in the lobby of a fancy hotel. I mean, it isn't against the law to eat in your room, right? We never did get room service; my mother always said they jacked up the price, and I wondered how my Uncle Jack had anything to do with price-fixing in hotels.

The next morning my mother did what she always did: woke

up early, pulled out and plugged in the electric frying pan that had been packed in my father's suitcase (because of course she did not want it in hers, crushing her suits), cracked a dozen eggs that my father had gone to a local store to purchase and we had kept in the cooler with fresh ice from the icemaker down the hall, and started breakfast. She fried the pound of bacon; the smell and the sizzling woke us up, the familiarity of the smoky aroma and the butter sliding beneath the eggs sheltering us in each other, fortifying us for our day ahead. We had paper plates that were in someone else's suitcase, I think one of the boys', and plastic forks and spoons brought from home.

My mom dished out eggs and bacon to each of us from the side table in the hotel room and we perched on the edges of both beds, some of us in chairs, some of us cross-legged on the floor. We didn't ever turn on the TV when we were eating—we were not that kind of family, though plenty of my friends' families were. They would sit in front of the television set like it was the great and powerful Wizard of Oz and no one would talk to each other.

We were still laughing about the cottage cheese, and I was laughing so hard I almost spit out my eggs, sitting cross-legged on the floor. That was before you knew how dirty hotel floors were—they sure didn't look it—or the news shows with the black light cameras showed you how gross the bedspreads were with all the splashes illuminated in purple lights and it could make you sick just thinking about it. But no, everything seemed clean and shiny and perfect, the curtains usually matching the bedspreads and the chairs in all three of our rooms looking exactly the same. Except the boys', whose room was messy almost as soon as they occupied it no matter what. My mother would have never let us sit on the floor if she thought it was dirty.

When the maid knocked on the door to see if everything was all right, we all laughed and my mother, said, "Yes, come back later." And we laughed pretty loud then too. It was lucky this was years before fire and smoke alarms in every hotel room because they surely would have gone off, and then what would we say? Likely we would have been asked to leave, and then where would the eight of us go? We would live on the street, that's what, because who would have time to send away for a brochure and wait for the response?

We cleaned up after ourselves, of course, and when the electric frying pan had cooled, my mother disposed of the grease in the toilet (that was probably not the right thing to do) and packed the pan away under shoes and jackets and hid the cooler in the closet. My mother had a full day planned for us, visiting Old Quebec with its churches and artists selling watercolor paintings on the street. I have a painting my mother bought that day, signed by an artist named "Mich." It is what my father called me; he had a sweet name for each of us, and he would say it with a certain melody that I can still hear if I concentrate, although he has been gone for thirty-one years.

That was my nickname, still is, and the watercolor was in our house for years. When my mother died eighteen years ago now, it naturally came to me. That and the fuchsia silk love seats, the two of them matching; they had been in my mother's living room. I loved them, and I begged for them when my sisters and I were dividing up all that was my mother's house on Ashland. I was expecting some kind of back-and-forth, to try to justify why I would get these glorious settees.

"No problem," Madeleine said. "They're hideous."

I pretended not to hear.

AFTER BREAKFAST AND CLEANUP, AND MAKING SURE WE ALL looked presentable (as if we were going to be "presented to monarchy," she'd say)—*who were we being presented to?* I always wondered—we set out on our adventure in a new city in a new country. Trying to be French. Madeleine dared me to ask a clerk in the lobby, "Quelle heure est-il?" because she said everyone spoke French and she loved teaching me things.

"It's nine-thirty," he responded in English.

It mattered what time it was always, even if I didn't have a watch, because my mother always said we had so much to do. We were always on a schedule, even had a scheduled nap time, which I think was more for my parents than for us. We had reservations for dinner. We would never be late.

But I liked to linger in the mornings, sitting on one of the hotel chairs pressed up against a writing desk; the smell of bacon lingering, all of us there, crowded, contained, our suitcases perched on the luggage racks. Our hotel room smelled like home.

LALA'S WEDDING

WE TALKED ABOUT COCELEBRATING FOR A ONE HUNDREDTH birthday, complete with dancing, karaoke, wine, cake, and most likely tiaras. I have a tank top I wanted to wear that says, "I feel precious about all my shit." I was set to turn sixty, and Sarah (or LaLa Land, her Roller Derby name) was turning forty. Together we have lived a century. Hence the one hundredth birthday.

We talked about perhaps having the party at her summer-house, the one a few blocks from Lake Michigan, that she and her husband bought with two other couples. She and Todd get the use of the cottage most weekends. The other couples work weekends or nights. Whatever food we would make—and we both love to cook for parties—would be vegetarian and there would definitely be pinot grigio. And ice.

We didn't get the chance to have the hundred-years birthday party because we both got busy with work and travel and family. But it was a funny thought.

I am not averse to getting older, I am surprised by it. I am not one of those women who is coy about her age and denies it; I am glad I am as old as I am. I am just not sure how long I will last. I feel a sense of urgency, though, like I am one of those darkening, tightening tangerines with the spotted skin in the fruit bowl in the breakfast room. Coming in close on my expiration date.

Maybe this is why I have a cadre of younger women friends. They make me feel like I might not die quite yet, that I have more adventures ahead.

LaLa gave me socks one Christmas, with "Mother Fucking Girl Power" in black letters on the sides. Sometimes I wear them under boots to meetings where I know I will be mansplained to, and sometimes I wear them to go for a walk.

We are not alike in more avenues than we are; LaLa is not like most of the women I have known for twenty and thirty years who feel like familiar habits, like brushing your teeth the same direction every night and morning or sleeping on your left side. They are the women who are my age and have the same woes about grown children and money and work and decaying homes, and most likely ex-husbands. It seems everybody has an ex-husband. Or a new one.

I am not LaLa's best friend. She has one of those, a lifelong friend since she was a little girl, Amanda. They are the same age, and they were friends when LaLa's mother died, and they were friends in grade school and high school and during and after college, and at each other's weddings and every birthday in between.

And I have a best friend, Dana. My roommate all during college, my best friend since then. She came in for our fortieth college reunion and stayed at my house except for the nights I booked a hotel room for us close to campus so I could drink and not worry about the drive home. I had only booked the first night, and Dana suggested we have a hotel room for the second night as well because there would be the football game and then more parties.

I balked at the price.

"I don't know, maybe you can spring for a hotel room every forty years with your best friend?"

DANA WAS RIGHT. SHE IS A THERAPIST NOW, AFTER YEARS AS AN actor and then an adult education teacher. Let me tell you how convenient it is to have your best friend who knows you down to your DNA be a therapist. Not that I take advantage, but she sure knows what to say when I don't know what to do. For that we do FaceTime.

Besides my three sisters, Dana is closest to my heart. Our friendship forged when we were becoming who we are, and we imprinted on each other. It is not just as we were developing our identities, it was as we were opening our minds, to new ideas and new ways to be in the world, pretending to be adults, performing as women, but not afraid to be smart, not afraid to be sexy, not afraid of much, or so it feels looking back at it all now. We also know all of each other's secrets, all of them. I think that is why both our ex-husbands were always wary of us.

We were not part of a tribe bigger than the two of us. We had other friends in college, of course, but we had each other, and whether it was in the third-floor apartment on Clark Street or the house on Sherman Avenue, the space we made for each other was accepting and open. Still is.

"I'M MARRYING SARAH," I WOULD TELL FRIENDS BEFORE HER September wedding. And sometimes I wouldn't explain.

When LaLa asked me to marry her, I knew what she meant. We were at a restaurant on Devon Avenue, a narrow place with an Indian vegetarian buffet that stretches along one wall—LaLa, Swati, me, Amanda, and Hell. That's short for Hellvetica, Stacy's derby name. We all had Roller Derby names; that's how we met, amateur Roller Derby on Tuesday nights. I am Mich the Masher.

It was six months before LaLa's wedding and we had met for one of our regular weekend brunches, organized with about seven or eight people at first, then sometimes down to just four. I love the paneer there—not so much the cubes of cheese, but the smooth spinach, warm and spicy. I made three trips to the buffet.

"Will you sit down and stop eating so I can ask you something!" LaLa blurted.

"Sure, what?"

"Will you marry me?"

I had never performed a wedding ceremony before, but she had it all figured out, the website where you get a certificate—you only have to pay online to become a universal minister. It even offers a parking pass (that's extra, though). You do have to register with the county, and she did have to get a marriage certificate I needed to sign. But there was no training, no screening process. So, yes. I can marry anybody now. Maybe not so surprising, but no one else has asked.

There's a comfort in an old friend who knows you as well as you know her, like a recipe you no longer have to consult a cookbook for or the one that is handwritten on an index card tucked in the blue wooden box in the pantry near the spices. The one with drips of vanilla or marinara sauce. The memories improve sometimes, enhanced mysteriously the way a college grade point average does on your résumé or an SAT score does forty years later.

I am lucky to have those friendships cultivated over two, three, four decades. I have a friend in her nineties, Ginny, and we've known each other almost forty years. Then there's my journalism tribe of women whose work I respect and admire and who would help me any day ever—and I would help them. Deborah, Teresa, Susy, Lisa, Amy, Katherine—these are women I work with, lead workshops with, travel with, cry with, consult when something goes bonkers or I have a question on where to go next with a story or how to respond to an editor. I learn from them and I hope can offer some wisdom in return. We go to each other's book signings and awards dinners and take loads of selfies.

There are the tribes of women as mothers of children in school, on teams; we go to weddings together, funerals, anniversary parties. Diane, Julie, Linda, Gail; we have talked and walked through each other's breathtaking family injuries and celebrations. We meet for dinner every few months—sometimes at the Italian place with the amazing meatballs on Thursday or Saturday nights featuring the singer who flirts with all the women, even if he does sing off-key.

There is no hiding. My friends know when something is terribly wrong—and they bring over dinner or wine, sometimes candles or gift certificates for a massage. I can be transparent and they will not judge.

"U OK?" is the only text they need to send to get an avalanche of honesty.

In 2016 I read about a study published in *Cancer* that researched the mortality rates of more than 9,000 women with breast cancer. Over ten years, there were 1,448 recurrences of the disease and 1,521 deaths, with 990 deaths directly attributable to breast cancer.

The researchers found that socially isolated women died more often. Women with a large social network didn't have the same death rates. Friends can keep you alive. I had breast cancer. I hope this is true.

LALA HAD A GIRLS' WEEKEND, A BACHELORETTE PARTY BEFORE her wedding, six of us, in Michigan for a wine-tasting tour. We climbed into the rented bus with two other groups of bachelorette parties, one bride in a plastic tiara. Those of us in LaLa's group were wearing matching pink "winosaur" T-shirts.

"Why do you have dinosaur T-shirts?" a young woman in a sundress holding a plastic cup filled with a Bloody Mary asked LaLa.

"We're paleontologists," she responded.

It was hard to keep coming up with paleontologist answers the rest of the day when they asked what we did exactly as paleontologists. We said it involved a lot of digging for bones. And that is very difficult work.

Newer friends do not have the insulation of collective faulty memory; we are not protected by bumper pads of time and distraction. Each meeting is fresh, and it matters how you are together each time, in the moment, because there is no safety of past to forgive or forget or revise. No automatic forgiveness. It makes you more careful.

LALA AND TODD CAME TO DINNER AT MY HOUSE MONTHS BEFORE their wedding. I made eggplant bake with marinara sauce, parmesan and sliced zucchini, mushrooms and red peppers because that's what LaLa likes. When we go out for Thai food, we always split spicy eggplant something.

Todd told me that night that only a few months after he and Sarah started dating, he bought a wedding ring for her. It was because the local jewelry store was going out of business and he knew that whenever the timing would work—a few years down the road, even—he would marry Sarah. I love that about Todd. Practical man with convictions.

I wrote that into the speech I gave at their wedding, when I married them. LaLa wanted a knot ceremony, so I had to look that one up, too. There were no knot ceremonies in the '80s when I got married. I worked hard to find exactly the right words and to express their love for each other because I found it sweet and sincere, and unlike what I knew when I was married.

My friendship with LaLa is not me reliving my thirties and forties again—no thanks. It's that sometimes I do not want to be only around women my age because I get tired of the same familiar points of view. I recall the time about six years earlier when we both randomly enrolled in Derby Lite in Oak Park and roller-skated on quad skates (with two wheels in front, two in back, not in a line like Rollerblades) almost every Tuesday night together, two hours of drills and races and relays in helmet, knee pads, wrist guards, and mouth guard, sometimes sequined hot pants, most always fishnets. My good friend Sue—Schmidtylicious— skated with us too, but she dropped out after a few years.

A group of us would go out for drinks after skating some nights, to that bar that was always crowded, in the Yorktown mall with the movie theater with the reclining seats, and it would likely be the highlight of my week. The waitresses were nice, and someone always ordered something to share—chips and salsa or jalapeno poppers. It felt good to make friends out of context: no promised loyalty, only genuine affection in the moment, not because of what you do or who you are but because you are funny when you skate.

Longevity is a good thing, but sometimes you need to let go and find new friends who reflect back to you what you may not see in yourself. And it may be the clearest view of all.

4

DRESS CODE

WEARING AN ABOVE-THE-KNEE FLORAL DRESS, I EMERGED FROM the dressing room in a wood and glass boutique store that smelled of lavender and the kind of candles forever flickering in spas and asked the sales associate, "Am I too old for this dress?"

It wasn't supershort, just in that in-between space where you would ask yourself—and maybe text a close friend with a photo—if, styled correctly, it was professional enough for a presentation. But I was alone and in a strange city, dawdling in the shop after dinner, and I have a bad habit, when I am alone and out of town, of buying clothes that don't quite fit into the rest of my life. I have the floppy hats to prove it.

"Well, how old are you?" she asked, earnest, even pensive.

"Fifty-five," I replied.

She seemed visibly shaken, her honest reaction to an abomination, as if I had just confessed to a gruesome crime years earlier and whispered to her where the evidence is buried.

"Oh, no, you just can't," she said and shook her head back and forth violently as if to signal that she would tell no one anywhere anytime even if pressed that I had against the rules of polite society tried it on.

Her stern rebuke implied I should take the dress off quickly and exit the store as soon as possible, without even so much as a glance at the accessories counter.

So I did.

I am surprised now that I was so easily dissuaded.

Six years later and reconciled with my own complicity during the Texas Boutique Incident, I refuse to accept age limits when it comes to my wardrobe or anyone else's. Yes, I am eligible for AARP, but I do not want to look like the accepted and prescribed cultural version of an older woman—the mythical old witch who lives in a shoe.

There is a deluge of reminders, from ads in magazines to clothing store displays, that women my age are not supposed to be allowed to dress the way we feel. Relegated to muted colors, shapeless knits, and long, flowing tunics, we can dillydally with accessories that are oversized and exaggerated well into our nineties, but we dare not think that we can get away with a form-fitting anything—even with head-to-toe Spanx underneath. We are ever reminded to stay in our predictable, old lady lane, to remain neutral, compliant and uncomplicated, for everyone else's comfort as much as our own.

These sartorial standards mimic the erasure foisted upon older women in what feels like every other arena of our lives. We are expected—and required—to be invisible, silent, absent in the classroom, conference room, boardroom, Congress, or any public arena in which we could be seen or heard.

But I will not go into that good night without a wardrobe fight. I am dressing for me, and I intend to express how I feel about myself (which is actually about thirty-seven). I am not age-defying or ageless, as the cosmetics industry demands I be; I am age-authentic.

Luckily, older women do have role models for fashion choices and style in two very recent additions to the sixties set: Madonna and Angela Bassett, both sixty-two, are undeniably fashionable, and joined by Christie Brinkley, who is sixty-six. Helen Mirren, Tina Turner, and Cher are rocking their seventies, while Jane Fonda and Rita Moreno demonstrate what the eighties look like without a care for the idea that we ought to blend into the crowd. Even if many of my style idols have been cosmetically enhanced—something I will never do.

There are also major social media influencers over fifty, women whose style and fashion consciousness earn them millions of followers and even more respect. Still, the *New York Times* referred to them as "Glamorous Grandmas"—a compliment sandwiched in a stereotype, especially since the article even noted that not all of its subjects were actually grandmothers.

Because of their megastar status and followings, none of these women are going to be remembered for wearing outfits that my friend Katie calls "going Mrs. Roper"—the muumuus and elastic-waisted pants that are supposedly the prescription uniform for women fifty and older, epitomized by the landlady on the 1970s–80s sitcom *Three's Company*.

I know many women of my generation say that age is the permission slip for the most deliciously liberating choice on the planet: to not give a damn what you look like anymore and slip into those flat, Velcro-closed shoes, pants without zippers, dresses shaped like housecoats with pockets, bras (once again) optional. If that liberates you, so be it; my stance is not judgmental.

But that choice is not for me.

I accept that I am no longer the twenty-one-year-old who wore tube tops and hot pants to class, but I can and will wear a flowered blouse with striped pants and a plaid jacket, mixing patterns like my younger colleagues do so well. I dress to mirror how vibrant I feel inside, and as an outward expression of my personal resistance to the old lady dress code.

At a birthday party for a younger neighbor recently, most of the women were luminous in their fitted sleeveless dresses, and the men—with gel-slicked hair, casual shirts, creased pants, and shoes with no socks—were laughing in clusters of confidence.

In a cobalt-blue halter top and white skirt with flower appliqués, I danced among them for almost three hours. After applauding the band for their last song, I walked home, slipped out of my emerald-green leather slides, and bounced upstairs to watch the news.

UNSEEN

GROWING UP, MY THREE OLDER SISTERS AND I PLAYED DRESS-UP with my mother's white half-slips, one of them a crinoline. Upon our heads, the elastic covering our ears, one slip served as wedding veil, another pulled up to our chests, and perhaps pinned under our armpits if needed, as the bodice of a wedding dress, and a third at our waists so it could be formal length. Likely we looked like cake decorations. Funny that we thought dressing like a bride was the ultimate costume fantasy—this was way before warrior princesses, mind you, it was the 1960s.

We never made our two brothers dress up as grooms—though it did cross our minds—and we played bride as often as we could. I think I was about four or five, it was definitely before I was in kindergarten, because it was in that time that for fun instead of dress-up, I begged my sister Madeleine to play "school" with me; I would sit at a desk in the basement while she played teacher, standing before me giving me words to spell.

"Neighbor" was one word I still remember reciting more than fifty-five years ago; I recall thinking that my sister was tricking me by adding a "g, " let alone an "h." But that was a decade before I took Latin and etymology in high school (my mother made us all do that) and I would mostly blindly believe what Madeleine told me, even if there were simmering doubts. It was our private in-home spelling bee. I believe she even passed out grades to her only pupil.

In the '60s and '70s, my grandma dressed up for bridge luncheons at the 19th Century Women's Club, and we all thought it was named that because all the ladies who went there for lunch were born in the nineteenth century.

My mother would pick my grandma up at her apartment on Wisconsin Avenue and Grandma would be waiting in the vestibule in her white gloves carrying her purse, wearing a hat usually, stockings—real stockings, I imagine the kind with the garter belt and a slip underneath a pretty dress that she made herself—and a fur coat if it was below 60 degrees.

And Grandma was always happy when we picked her up to drop her off, smiling through her lipstick. I sat in the back seat of the cranberry-colored Lincoln convertible that my mom loved to drive. My legs were swinging from the cream leather seat, and it was before seat belts were the law, so I slid across the seat when my mom made wide turns. And my mom and my Grandma loved each other—you could tell—because they talked and laughed in shorthand.

"Oh, Mother," my mom would say if Grandma cracked a joke, and my mom would seem less like a mom than a daughter and a best friend, and it made me hungry. Hungry for what, I don't know, but maybe I just wanted somebody to talk to me that way, in a knowing, secret language for two. Both of them dressed up for the world—my mother wore skirts and blouses most all of the time—and smiling, checking off the tasks and days with cheer.

"Mrs. B" is what my father called my grandma, short for Mary

Butler. My dad was kind to her, a gentleman always, pulling the chair out for her at every meal and carrying things for her to and from the car. I think it's because he missed his own mother; I never knew her, she died in her fifties, before I was born.

Grandma never openly surrendered to her demise, even in the very end, when she was eighty with heart disease and not doing well. She was at our house most every night for dinner and before she went into the hospital for the last time. My mom was still helping her put bobby pins in her silver hair that was soft as the silk dresses she made me.

My mother didn't white flag it either, never surrendered to the dress code of older women with grandchildren. She was ordering St. John suits from Neiman Marcus until she went into the hospital, those three months before she died. My sisters and I would wash and curl her hair in the hospital, and then in the hospice room. In the very end, she didn't bother to wear the bathrobe with the butterflies on it. I have it now.

It was my grandmother who gave me a peek into the construction of a garment and how you can create from scratch how you will look—all your choice, no grabbing from a rack with scores of sameness and repetition. You could imagine who you wanted to be. And Grandma could make it happen—at least on the outside.

Grandma made my Aunt Paula's wedding dress; it was shiny and white and perfect. I walked down the aisle in front of her—my mother's youngest sister—wearing a pale yellow silk dress with a cream underslip shell and white embroidered butterflies on the collar. I was a flower girl, five years old, carrying a basket of daisies. White patent leather Mary Janes to match, white anklets with lace folded over.

My grandmother also made my dress for senior prom, followed a month later with my ivory jersey graduation dress—that still hangs in my closet, though it is unlikely I could ever fit into it again. My prom dress was apricot silk—likely it was polyester—and it had a sweetheart neckline with a halter top, ties at the neck. I picked out a pattern and the fabric with my mother at the local fabric store, now long gone, having given way to a coffee shop with a barista.

I loved the thump thump thump of the bolt of fabric with yards unfolding at the hands of the salesperson who always seemed to have a yellow measuring tape around her neck and scissors in the pocket of her apron. That sound signaled the dream of infinite glamour. It was about transformation and imagining what could be. In my grandmother's hands, deft and precise, this shiny pile of fabric tucked into a paper bag would make me a princess. Maybe even loved.

To go with the dress, Grandma made me an ostrich-feathered shawl with a tie in the center, having informed me that a simple boa would look cheap, but if she sewed the feathers onto an off-the-shoulder wrap, it would be elegant. She improvised the shawl without a pattern, and the peach-colored feathers matched perfectly.

I pictured myself as irresistible as the thin-waisted actresses sipping cocktails and descending staircases in the black-and-white movies I watched on TV late at night, lying on the floor of the family room, on a pillow with a blanket, enchanted. Even though it was 1975, I wanted some crumb of the elegance I imagined I could have, whether or not someone would spill beer on it at a secret party in someone's basement when the parents weren't home before we ever got to the prom.

My grandmother was a genius at the sewing machine; the gift of her making me a dress—particularly when she had twenty-six other grandchildren—was miraculous. I knew because of her I would not look like anyone else that night. I credit the years of insufferable Catholic school uniforms—I still wince at black watch plaid—with my unquenchable desire to look different from anyone else in the room.

In high school I cared so much about what I wore that I diagrammed my outfits for the week, careful not to repeat the lavender velvet pants or the corduroy monster bell-bottom jeans within that prescribed seven-day stretch. I loved my six-inch red suede ankle-strap platforms that I saved to buy at Giggles boutique. My mother said I could not wear them to school, so I wore gym shoes out the door and later changed into the red suede platforms stashed in my bookbag. I was taller and more slender in those shoes; I was rebellious.

In college no one was there to tell me what to wear, and I was enchanted by the clothes my roommate Dana wore; she was from New York, an Andover grad who was preppy and East Coast urban at the same time. I did my best not to look or act "all Midwest" and made friends with stylish New York girls like Hillary and Michele and carefully concocted a disco wardrobe and a sexy student wardrobe; I loved my pencil-thin turquoise pants and wore them with a fuchsia tunic and huge earrings the size of small donuts.

After college, I wanted to look more sophisticated than I was, older, smoother, more European I guess, or at least more like the women I saw in the pages of *Vogue, Elle, Bazaar*. On a trip to Italy with my friend Mariann after college, I deliberately adopted a different persona, wearing scarves and a hat and bearing a saunter that was definitely borrowed, not owned.

"You're not Italian, OK, so just stop," she said.

In my twenties, I worked for newspapers, magazines, and a fashion trade paper, and wrote a weekly feature on fashion as a freelancer for the *Chicago Sun-Times*. My editor, Patricia Shelton, was a kinder and appreciably gentler version of Miranda Priestly in *The Devil Wears Prada*, twenty-six years before the movie made the innards of a fashion publication a pop culture joke.

Pat had a cigarette-smothered voice, and her blonde hair was neatly coiffed in a bob. She looked out of place in the dusty, cluttered, fourth-floor newspaper offices on Wabash Avenue. When I would go to her desk to deliver my typed stories, she had me wait while she edited.

Thanks to her, I interviewed designers and attended fashion shows, furiously taking notes and trying to compare colors to fruit and artwork recalled from Art History class. Paloma Picasso was the most elegant person I had ever met or interviewed.

I remember thinking and believing that fashion was not everything, but it was something more than what you wore, an expression of self, a declaration of a dream, an intention of who you wanted the world to believe you were. You could feel seen.

At the annual designer sales at Marshall Field's, I'd be thrilled if a skirt, blouse, or jacket bore a designer label and a price tag that had been crossed out in red many, many times with a new price about 10 percent of the original, which was all I could afford.

When I was a feature writer at the *Dallas Times Herald* in the 1980s, I also wrote a weekly fashion column, interviewing designers, writing about trends. I loved asking them about their inspirations and hearing in their words not why a certain color or shape was the latest fad but what inspires them. Stuart Weitzman was smart and somewhat nerdy; Ralph Lauren had a slight lisp.

My thirties, forties, and fifties are a blur of working parenthood and neat jackets befitting a journalist, professor, and author. I still wear the blue wool military cropped jacket with the gold buttons—though long ago I took out the shoulder pads. It was the first jacket I bought after my oldest son was born. I bought it for his christening; I was so excited to wear something with a waist. It doesn't look so bad with jeans.

I have subscribed to *Vogue* for forty years, and even though most every page is filled with something I do not believe real people wear in real life, I do like to see the inspirations from the runway, the mixes of color, the patterns, the adornments, the final touches. Each new issue is a promise, a peek into what is new and fresh and stylish, at least what a handful of editors declare to be so. I like the essays and book reviews, the photos of magnificent gardens.

I like the feel of scarves around my neck, wrapping myself in the silk or wool scarves passed down from my mother, some others from friends, some I bought for myself when I was in a certain mood, some from who knows where.

When I am at a party with people I have never met, attending a meeting for an organization where I know no one, at a conference getting coffee, sitting alone at the big white table laid out for breakfast, I feel invisible. On the escalator, on the commuter train headed downtown reading my emails on my phone, I am just another old lady. Nothing ahead of her. Everything behind.

Yet sometimes a stranger will comment, "I like your scarf." Sometimes it's my shoes.

6

NEGATIVE SPACE

I WAIT BY THE SIDE DOOR ON MONROE STREET IN THE LINE TO the right for members; the sky is cellophane clear and the steel buildings lining Michigan Avenue to the west lean into its blueness. A young girl with cranberry-colored hair and dressed all in black is texting. A mother and father with fidgeting children in T-shirts and gym shoes adjust the youngsters like salt and pepper shakers on a diner's counter. The uniformed guard is smiling but firm on not opening the door a minute before 10:30.

It is Saturday morning and at the start of sketch class at the Art Institute of Chicago where the instructor, Mark, who sometimes wears a cravat, sings, "Bonjour!" at the start of his lecture.

We respond in chorus. Mine in a similar lyrical tone pretending I am French, even though I have only been to France twice, though to Canada much more often. I could speak French *un petit peu* (a little bit) in college, having taken a few quarters of conversational texts, and could read a book in French, understanding maybe half of it. Maybe 30 percent. I know what cornichons are. And they are delicious.

In a skillful twenty-minute talk, Mark defines *negative space* and shows examples on slides in Ryan Auditorium where thirty or so of us artists in varying degrees of gray amateurishness gather. I wait like a seal for a thrown minnow to grasp what Mark says. He is so insightful, I nearly swoon.

I sit in the front row, near a woman who calls me Melissa every week, as she has done for the last three years. I have stopped correcting her.

I listen intently, my phone turned to silent. I nod and try to absorb every word, taking it in fully as if it is some magical sustenance only for me. He is finished with the lecture and now we are at the back of the auditorium, with our clipboards and our plastic mesh supply bags, waiting to take a sheet or two of gray paper.

We wait in a jagged line as he tells us to use only white pastel for the assignment. I am usually ahead of the group, eager to begin. I wear my linen apron caked with charcoal and pastels, and I make my way to the storage cabinet where the assistant instructor, Barbara, is waiting, to the right of the main marble staircase, moving mostly in silence, or sometimes chatting with hollow pleasantries like strangers in an elevator. I say thank-you when she reaches out with a folding chair and move across to the assigned gallery.

I adjust my gray plastic seat in Gallery 201, European Painting and Sculpture, parking perhaps five feet in front of the French impressionist Gustave Caillebotte's most famous work, *Paris Street; Rainy Day*. I try to avoid being jostled by the blue and black backpacks of the dozens of tourists, gazers, and lovers immobile and transfixed by its size (about 7 by 9 feet) and the familiarity of its images (a top-hatted man and well-dressed woman strolling near others shielded by umbrellas on a rain-slicked cobblestone street.

Cradling my clipboard, with my pastels and eraser nestled in my aproned lap, I strain to see the master work differently, honoring what is behind and under and above the outlines, finding meaning in the aftermath and the pauses of the gestures. Do not draw an outline. You cannot draw what is obviously there. Draw what is not. The solid objects will emerge if you draw what is in between.

The repetition of shapes between figures and buildings expose what is not measurable, what bears no depth. I assign it the shape it deserves with the end of a white pastel crayon, the dust of my strokes littering the paper.

This is my rescue, my refuge, my respite. No one is calling, texting, emailing, asking me to meet a deadline, edit a story, file a report, deposit money, pay a bill, fix an error, attend a meeting, or respond to questions I have no answer for.

I HAVE BEEN WORKING SINCE I WAS SIXTEEN. COLLEGE, GRADUATE school, jobs in journalism, eighteen years working at a university. Marriage. Motherhood. As soon as my oldest son was born, I felt I was fully spoken for. I stopped being able to do anything that wasn't a necessity. Two more sons in five more years. One less husband. A career that required time and intellectual energy and got increasingly more splintered and complicated with multiple bosses to answer to, perform for, maneuver around capriciously so as not to ignite a negative reaction.

I stopped painting, sketching, creating art; there was simply no room in between the requirements of maintaining a family, a house, a résumé. For decades I had not been able to make time for anything much beyond work, home, family, and volunteering for causes that I believe strongly need my help. Five nonprofits where I am on the advisory boards.

SOMETIMES THE PEOPLE IN THE MUSEUM TALK TO ME—INTERRUPT is more like it, but I know they are just trying to be nice, supportive, give me a compliment. I sketch quietly, intent, with a surgeon's focus on each line I draw, each sweep of my thumb. Little girls breaking away from their parents come up to my folding seat and stand so close I can feel their breath, so I know they must feel safe.

"That is so good," says the girl in the sneakers, until her mother tells her to leave me alone.

Sometimes people just stand near me and stare at my drawing; they do the same to the other people in the class who are sprinkled throughout the galleries like paprika. Careful not to get too close to the paintings or the sculptures for whatever the assignment is for the day, I smile at the museum guards, who smile back. Sometimes they chat with me and ask me how long I have been drawing.

"I did not sketch for twenty-five years," I say, and they act surprised.

I love these hours in the galleries. It is selfish; it is the space for myself in between that I never had all those years. It is mine. Now this space is mine. Every Saturday—except for the breaks between the classes. The two weeks off make me anxious.

I AM LUCKY. I AM LUCKY. I AM LUCKY.

I hear the mantra I speak as if it is coming from the lips of someone else. I feel this when I am not in class: this is when I am worried; this is a sizable portion of the rest of my life.

I worry about money a lot. I worry about my work, if it will continue, if I can sustain this level of output. I worry about my sons. I worry about my health. I worry about my brothers' and sisters' health. And then there are headlines and shocking new realities that make me worry about everything, including the future of the planet, humanity, oh, yes, and democracy. There's that.

The uneasiness starts as a steady rocking deep within the skeleton of my hands and arms, as if my buried muscles and cells are tingling; not deep shaking, but more like a vibration sent by the wind, a silent sweep. I feel it in my head and my neck. The vibration offers a sense of detachment, as if I am watching myself go through motions, this vibration reminding me that I am exiled. Out of myself.

But not in a way that is restful or pleasant, an escape. This is a banishment from myself, like Napoleon in Elba, away from Josephine. I am not allowed to take up the full space I have made for myself. I am a squatter, watching the owner move through her tidy, organized, uninterrupted life.

It comes and goes, stays for stretches of days, maybe weeks. Always when I am under severe stress. It has been several weeks now, watching my feet move beneath me, almost as if I am watching myself from above, perched on a ladder, listening to myself as if it is a third person.

In the early evenings when I go for a walk, I see my feet move below me in my white-and-green running shoes on the nearby college track and through the neighborhood where I stare at the gardens—some meticulous, some weed-filled—and try to name the flowers. I see the curtains in the windows, I see the men sitting alone watching baseball games on enormous TVs, the women cooking in kitchens while children sit at the table on cell phones. The recyclable bags of clippings on the lawns that will be picked up on time in the morning as promised.

There is the house with the evergreen bushes forced into manicured shapes that look like skateboards. The white plastic fence barricades intruders from the outdoor, in-ground pool surrounded by empty lawn chairs, lined neatly like tiny toy soldiers on the perimeter. There is a television on the wall, and no one is watching the images flickering across the enormous screen.

I reach out to feel the fences and the trees and hold the leaves in my right hand to see if I can feel them. I can. I am not lost completely.

Throughout the day most days of the week I am watching myself type, drink coffee, participate in conferences, all as if on a three-second delay. I go to dinner with friends and hear myself speak and laugh. I wonder whether the sadness is leaking and my friends say for all I am feeling I could look so much worse. I say thank-you and watch the words fly across the room as if they were mailed by a stranger.

I am sometimes waiting to get back into register, shoved back into myself. I know that it happens as quickly as the removal. I have not yet arrived into my body. It passes. As I said, it comes and goes. I know it will go.

THE PASSPORT DREAM HAPPENED AGAIN LAST NIGHT. I HAVE meticulously packed and am headed to the airport in a car with work friends—always a different group, sometimes my sisters— when I look in my purse and see that I do not have my passport. My heart pounds and I tell everyone I need to get out and to go back and that I will meet them there. The car keeps going, I keep insisting, and I am mentally calculating the feasibility of getting back home, going to the drawer where my passport is, and making it back to the airport in time for TSA. I even remind myself I am preapproved and try to imagine whether there is enough time. I am always with a group of people who are fully prepared—who each have their passports—and who seemed surprised I do not have mine. They will not let me out of the car.

The dream ends differently each time—but it never ends with me having my passport in hand successfully boarding the plane en route to the intended destination, which is sometimes a work trip and sometimes a glorious vacation, always to another continent.

Sometimes in the dream I get to the airport and stand in line after checking my bags only to be told by the TSA official that I can go no further. Once I was as far along as getting on board the plane and in my seat and was taken off by an agent because they discovered I had no passport. You don't have to have a psychology degree to figure out the meaning that even with the best of plans, I cannot get to where I am going. This is not what I planned for, I am missing something. I am blocked from moving ahead to my destination.

It is me who has fallen short. I forgot the passport. No one took it from me, no one barred me from including it in my bag. I was lacking. And so I get denied the trip, the future—oh, come on, this is pretty damn transparent. Because of my own doing, it never turns out as I dreamed.

IN THE WHITE BLOTCHES OF SHADING ON THE GRAY PAPER, THE spaces between reveal the action and the movement, the solid presence of men and women and the buildings they slide past. When you surrender to observing this way, it is difficult to readjust. The space between a couple's bodies asserts a new definition of what is there. The deliberate position of a roof and an umbrella calibrate a different aesthetic, and I see that the importance of what is not drawn is as important as what is.

When I am done, the sketch looks different from one I might have made if I had drawn it traditionally, with outlines and details, filling in shadows. And it is not just because it is white and gray with the objects on the bare paper and the pastels swirling around them. Now the space between has more substance than the objects themselves.

The two hours are up. Mark leans over my shoulder and sighs, "Oh my. That is so nice." He acts surprised by my sketches every week, or so he says, and he looks at them with a parent's doting. I find myself longing for his approval, and when he suggests I add a swipe of white or a smudge of green, I do what he says because he is always right. And this is the in-between space where no one knows who I am and no one knows the weighty mess of my six and a half other days of the week. Today's class has me looking beyond and between at everything.

Today I am no one's mother. I am no one's editor. I am no one's mentor and no one's employee. I do not have to keep quiet on conference calls where I disagree with the directions given. I have no deadline, other than the one suggested by Mark, who will call us back to the studio for us to critique our work.

In a painting or sketch it's the area between objects, not the outlines of the solid objects themselves. In the negative space— that is, the between part—the air, the shadows, the translucent nonpresence become animated and hallucinatory. A kind of Rorschach test of visuals, you discern what is there by examining what isn't. Reorienting to that point of view is a relief, a discovery. The nothingness grows its own weight.

If you draw the negative space, you are conscious that it is a reversal, that it is not logical, that it is not the way others move through the world, reserving their reverence for what is there, not for what is not. But sometimes the objects and the events and the bodies of what bears weight in your view is no longer bearable. You look at the lines between trees and vases and fruit and flowers and lovers for what is important and memorable, and you soon do not see the substance of the weight of what everyone else sees first.

The negative space is where you can float.

☆ PART TWO ☆

WORK

APPLAUSE

MY SCRIPT IS PRINTED IN 16-POINT TIMES NEW ROMAN, double-spaced, in case I forget to bring my dollar-a-pair cheater reader magnifying glasses to the podium. The end of each page is the end of the paragraph, with no staples on the pages; I want to seamlessly move through the speech without fussing and turning pages over midsentence, midthought, bending the script.

Instead I slide each page quietly, almost unnoticed, to my left on the dais when I am finished. I don't memorize these half-hour or hourlong speeches, there are too many details I could miss; I know because I have missed them.

I don't improvise. I have learned that lesson. Years ago, before a conference in Chicago, I switched briefcases at the last minute and left the printed-out speech at home in the abandoned briefcase. Much scrambling and panicking ensued before I could reach my oldest son to email the document to my cell phone. But oh, that type was small.

Yes, I have witnessed many, many people who can step to the lectern with, "I will just speak off the top of my head," but hearing that when I'm in the audience makes me roll my eyes and squirm. It's like asking someone over to your home for dinner and then announcing upon your guest's arrival that you will just open the cupboards and see what's there—oh, look, oatmeal! Some radishes in the veggie bin too, and moving on to the fridge, how about this leftover pizza from last Wednesday? How special.

If I have been invited as a keynote speaker, I will deliver—and cash the check—because I love this part of my life. And I understand that "love" is a big word, but I love to stand up in front of strangers to perform a part. I am hungry not just for acceptance but, in the words of Sally Field, I want them to like me, to really like me. I need the affirmation.

I also do live storytelling, even going so far as the Moth Grand-SLAM event in Chicago; mostly the live stories I do are with storytelling groups hosted in bars where people have alcohol and maybe because of that think I am funny. I like that their laughter temporarily fills me, an antidote to much else in my life that is criticized, scrutinized, and not met with any brand of amusement.

And I know how to get the affirmation—from the stage anyway—plotting and planning how to say what I have to say in the most artful way possible so they like me. I want anyone, everyone to like me. I understand this is why many of my friends date as hectically as they do, but I don't need it so much from strange men. I can attribute that to having far too many trust issues, but this need feels like it can be quashed more safely. A room full of strangers can applaud what I offer in the course of an hourlong speech or story and it will make my day, maybe my week. Sometimes it makes my year, until the next big speech comes along.

I love the applause at the end. I love the applause at the beginning too, after I am introduced, the anticipation, of OK, let's see what she's got, though I know many audience members already have formed an opinion from my bio in the program at the tables. That is more blind generosity than really earning a hearty clap. I applaud mightily when someone else takes the stage, to provide a little encouragement—here ya go, it will be fine, go for it! Because I want them to do well, I always do. And I want to do well. Yes, I aim to please. Though I do always picture myself bombing. I work hard to avoid that feeling of catastrophe.

I love the bursts of claps in the middle of my speech too. I am an approval hoarder; I seek it, I crave it, I want to be appreciated. This is not my highest priority in life, but it is in the top ten. Above hot bath, below getting a clean bill of health at the doctor and a reduced rate on my mortgage, and a few other things that I cannot mention here because I have three grown sons who may read this book.

My extroverted need for attention does not stem from pathology—at least I hope not, and the many therapists I have seen for fifty minutes at a time with or without insurance coverage never said it was—nor a tragic childhood where I was ignored. I had a pretty great childhood, not perfect or idyllic but close; there just were a lot of us—six in seven years. So my parents had limited one-on-one time, a practical necessity. This was decades before helicopter parenting; that was unheard of (also would have been impossible: not enough helicopters to go around).

A few years back I saw the award-winning movie *Lady Bird*, about a mother and daughter in a fraught relationship. They are arguing at the resale shop, arguing in the car, laughing in the kitchen, and sometimes the exchanges are cruel and acrid. But all I could think as I watched was that I never had that kind of consistent alone time with my mother. I wanted to, and I craved being acknowledged not as one in a group of "well-behaved children in such a big family!" by strangers but just alone, for me. I was acknowledged, we all were, but there is only so much time and attention in a day for six.

Maybe "never" is too strong a word for how often I was alone with my mom, but I cannot remember more than a few incidents where it was just me. I took walks alone with my father on the beach in Long Beach, Indiana, on the weekends in the summers in my teens and twenties because my mother was always cooking the next meal at our house with the deck filled with a dozen lounges and mismatched plastic cushions the colors of sunflowers and roses. I didn't know then that my father would die soon from a stroke or I would have made sure those walks were longer.

As a family, my brothers and sisters and I did a lot with one another and with our parents—vacations, trips to the movies, out to dinner, mostly at the golf club, Riverside, because the other clubs closer to our house did not allow Roman Catholics. Riverside was where the waitresses brought orange cheese dip and glass trays of radishes, celery, pickles, and those tasteless black olives with the holes in the center that come from a can. The first time I tasted real olives from Spain I was so surprised— sort of like your first real great kiss, when you suddenly understand, oh, so *this* is what the fuss is all about, and it's nothing like it looks on *The Love Boat*.

The six of us were together a lot of the time. Our parents were with us a lot. "Quality time," it was later called, and when we each grew up to have our own children—collectively the six of us have twenty-one children, and those children have eighteen children of their own—my generation was admonished to spend quality time with our kids. As children of the '60s, we were told that to seek out individual attention was to be spoiled; you were a brat, conceited. And none of us wanted to be that. Actually, being bratty was not allowed.

So it was not such a good or noble thing that I craved attention from family as well as strangers. I guess it is just vain, selfish, and shallow, how much I liked attention. My need never prompted me to do anything risky and life-threatening, though I did date men I should not have and married one I should not have for sure. But yes, I coveted innocent smiles from strangers—a group of them is best—for a performance, an idea, a speech, an article, anything I could make or do or be, and that filled me, or at least a part that seemed always emptying or empty. Noticed. Get noticed.

IT WAS THE SUMMER OF 1967, AND MY TASK WAS TO FIGURE out how to design a curtain that would hang across the driveway on Augusta Street so no one would get a free peek.

My across-the-street neighbor, Mary (who lived in the red-brick house with her brothers and parents and grandparents) and I had produced, rehearsed, and choreographed our first ever roller-skating show. It was an extravaganza that involved costumes and daredevil feats of each of us skating in circles and jumping over broom handles—a sort of obstacle course before that was a reality show thing. I was nine.

We sold tickets for fifty cents each and promised that Mary's mom would be baking treats for the audience. She was probably the biggest draw; her cookies and brownies were locally famous. She made a cake for the event and cut it into squares so people could eat it with their hands, no forks.

In the weeks leading up to the roller-skating show, Mary and I had gone door-to-door—she went down Jackson, I went down Monroe, knocking, ringing doorbells to sell the idea that this would be a demonstration of expertise the likes of which our neighborhood had never seen. I think we sold about twenty tickets, and then we had to figure out how many people could fit on a picnic bench, as three of the benches were lined up under the basketball hoop.

Our Saturday morning show was billed as so extraordinary that I imagined passersby would want to park and sneak a view, without paying the admission. There were no trees close enough to the driveway to hang up sheets to prevent nonpaying customers from viewing the show. So I abandoned the idea of privatizing the driveway, even though it was a precursor to the idea of a paywall that was yet to emerge.

Mary wore a clown costume and I wore red lipstick I had filched from my mother's makeup drawer. The roller-skating show featured Mary and me skating back and forth in the driveway, dipping and swaying on our quad skates for about thirty minutes to a selection of 45s spinning on the record player in the garage with the help of many, many extension cords.

The audience of about ten neighbors and siblings applauded heartily. I felt like Cher, without the singing, flat stomach, or flimsy costumes. I was in the spotlight, so to speak, but people were looking at me and I was loving it, even if my sisters appeared bored. Mary's mother was in the audience, I think my mom watched from the window; it was just one more thing I was doing on a calendar of look-at-me efforts. I also one summer painted landscape scenes on small rocks and sold them from a stand in front of the house.

The applause was good. I went to bed that night feeling deeply pleased with myself.

Growing up I did think briefly about how it might be if I were an only child, like my friend Jennifer, whose parents doted on her as if she were a princess. Jennifer had enormous stuffed animals in her bedroom—life-sized dogs with floppy ears bigger than she was, and her mother kept checking on us if I went to her house on Park Avenue to play.

Jennifer always had new clothes, not hand-me-downs like I had from my sister Madeleine. Oh, not everything was handed down—I did get some new clothes, but mostly my clothes were not mine first. Bikes either.

I remember saying that when I grow up I am going to buy a bike for myself, one that is new, not with scuffed tires, a faded leather seat, or a worn basket. It will have a shiny new bell and I will be the first to ring it. I did get a new bike when I was thirteen. My father took me to the Sears at the corner of North and Harlem for it, and it was a bright yellow ten-speed and I thought I was the coolest thing.

In high school I longed for attention and was a real suck-up to all the teachers because it mattered to me that in a class of thirty—yes, it was about thirty to a class back then—I wanted to be seen. I raised my hand a lot and said, "Oh! Oh! Oh!" when I knew the answer, madly waving at the teacher, who mostly ignored me to give others a chance. I get that now, but at the time it only made me raise my hand and moan more.

My brother Paul told me once when I complained about not getting called on that I should try to trick the teacher and act bored, look around the room, pretend I was not paying attention, and then I'd get called on. Paul said this was reverse psychology. It worked.

TONIGHT AS I PREPARE TO DELIVER MY SPEECH, I AM WATCHING myself on screens hoisted high throughout the ballroom as if I were a baseball player at bat in the World Series. But there is no sportscaster announcing my wins and losses, how many times I have been traded, and if this is a good season or not.

I am standing straight, wearing my favorite keynote necklace—sparkling gray baubles too many and too big a statement for anything more private and less public than this. I had worried about my hair and my shoes and the dress—though at the last minute I left the carefully chosen ivory jacket at my seat at the head table.

Writing the words I will say before this audience took twenty times longer than saying them. When I craft a speech, I am mindful of plucking the words carefully, like picking raspberries willfully and deliberately. Sometimes the words are ready to be placed into sentences, sometimes they are not, and you get scratched by the thorns. Yet, sometimes the words are just right.

I've been delivering speeches like this for about twenty years and I try hard to say something to make people laugh, gasp, sigh, or feel something emotionally stirring—shock, maybe empathy or horror. I have learned how to slow down, pause—letting silence blow into the room like an unexpected wind. I watch TED Talks on YouTube for inspiration and do my best to deconstruct why and how each phrase worked well, and I know never ever to sprinkle my speech with *ums*.

From where I stand, the audience of about four hundred people, well dressed in sequins or suits for an evening fund-raiser, is quiet at first, some still sipping their wine or after-dinner drinks or playing with the dessert on the plate—sometimes a mousse, lately parfaits, or cakes (the ice cream sundae craze is over, thank God). A few minutes into my talk, they are silent.

The room is festooned with silver and white balloons and careful floral arrangements that reach above the guests so the flowers do not inhibit conversation. I keep talking, making eye contact with as many strangers as I can as I scan the tables. Sometimes the spotlight makes it impossible for me to see those in the back. But I move my head and look in all directions, a sweep, as I am speaking, to make sure I leave no one out.

I have practiced this speech in my office—the family room—and in the shower, in my bedroom before bed, in the car, dozens and dozens of times. The actual speech in real time feels like it's in slow motion. But I am waiting to get to the end when what I am living for tonight is the applause and the feeling it brings me.

The applause is choppy and fast, quick syncopation, matching the pulsing in my ears. Sometimes everyone is standing at the end and each time, each and every time, chills spread up my arms, tingling the hairs. I am shamelessly bathing in the clapping flow, soaking in it, measuring my worth in its duration. The applause gives me a transfusion of confidence, even if just for the duration of the evening.

I really love the applause.

I am high, invincible, if only for a few short minutes. It's an illusion, I know, but I feel connected to everyone in the room, we are sharing this moment, though it is my triumph to claim because I have spilled a secret or touched on a truth in a way they had not thought of saying. It feels narcissistic, it feels joyous, I am jubilant. I maybe love it more than I should.

This is the feeling you can get from winning a raffle or having great sex because it's temporary, but for the moment it's thorough and cell-fueling and glorious. But as shiny as it is, it is a thin sunlight, or moonlight, or both, diaphanous and elusive, as it vaporizes in a very short while.

When I walk back to my seat, I take a gulp of the wine that has been untouched in my glass all evening. A stream of guests at other tables come up to introduce themselves and say how much it meant what I said, and I feel like Miss America getting rushed on stage by all the other contestants—though I don't believe in beauty contests. I take their business cards. Sometimes they want something, sometimes they don't, and I usually cannot remember them, though I try.

This experience is not sustainable because it is not reciprocal; it is one-way. This is not the joy of a thirty-year-old friendship or a son walking across a stage to reach for a diploma and pointing toward you in the bleachers. This is not an "I love you" that makes you cry when you think of it in all its tender brokenness because you know your response is the same.

I chase it nonetheless—the applause. Like a fool, like someone lonely and insecure who works alone on her laptop eleven hours a day in the family room that she calls an office. Because that is what I do. I wonder if needing the acknowledgment so much signals how little I value myself for myself. If the oxygen other people breathe into me is only what resuscitates me, that I cannot sustain myself. And yes, that is pathetic.

And try as I always do, I cannot sustain it. The applause withers, I go home or back to my hotel room with the key card that I never can seem to get to spark the green light on the first try, inside where there are just a few too many pillows on the bed and never enough conditioner in the teeny tiny bottles in the bathroom. Lately the shampoo and the conditioner smell like mint and remind me of mouthwash.

I hang up my fancy clothes and take off the shoes that invariably hurt, and I smile to myself that I did it. Again. Going over in my head the lines that went well, the lines that maybe didn't go as well as I thought and try to see what I could do better next time. Because I am always thinking about the next time. I need the next time.

From the ninth floor or the third or, God forbid, the room across from the elevators or next door to the loud couple arguing, I am trying my best to grasp onto this gelatinous feeling that what I do matters to someone other than me. I am hanging with a death grip onto the notion that I am filled up, that I am enough. The applause has made me feel good enough as I am. For a moment.

It's quiet in the room so I put on my yoga pants and the silk camisole I wear to bed, and I turn on that HGTV show about island houses where the wife complains that the doorknobs are wrong and the deck is too small and the husband stands there smiling while the realtor tap-dances for her approval.

It's never enough for some people.

8

ON PURPOSE

THE LYRICS IN PEGGY LEE'S "IS THAT ALL THERE IS?" SEEMED as inscrutable to me as she was; but it was 1969 and I was eleven—what did I know of the world, of anything—watching this honeyed-voiced guest on one of the many television variety shows I watched in the family room.

"Is that all there is? Is that all there is? If that's all there is, my friends, then let's keep dancing. Let's break out the booze. And have a ball."

The refrain stuck with me because I disagreed; I thought the meaning of life surely could not be booze and dancing, though I could make a case for the dancing then and now.

Today in my seventh decade, I am viewing the work I do in my life as more finite than I have—ever. Fourteen years a cancer survivor, I am not a half-empty type, but I am realistic; I had the type of breast cancer that comes back. And I need to go back every six months to the dermatologist because of a precancerous blotch my doctor scraped off my chest during a skin check.

At my annual mammogram recently, I spilled tears of anticipation when I signed my name at the front desk of the eighth-floor office. It was here in 2006 that a routine checkup found my cancer, without symptoms, without indications.

I was only relieved recently when the doctor explained while showing me the 360-degree views—the thorough views that insurance does not cover completely—that there was no change, I was fine and likely to survive many more years. No, thank you, Peggy Lee, my instinct was not to break out the booze and dance in resignation. Because I am trying my best to have more than this.

Purposefulness, mindfulness, meaning—these are multimillion-dollar buzzwords for my generation, worthy of conferences, webinars, guidebooks, coaches, consultants, counselors, TED Talks, and keynotes. Finding meaning and purpose fills bookshelves and endless podcast lists.

I am not alone in my self-questioning—an extension of the persistent imposter syndrome, I gather—that whatever I have done or will do may never be enough. In my work I have mentored women who are MacArthur "genius grant" winners, founders of organizations, and CEOs of companies all who fail to mention it in their bios because they feel it would be too much to take in, it would feel braggadocious.

I know there are always and forever those whose imprint on the world and history are infinitely larger than mine; Antoni Gaudí's Sagrada Família cathedral in Barcelona comes to mind, as does Nikole Hannah Jones's 1619 Project. I know what I have done but am reminded more of what I have not done. I know so much of what I am not qualified to do.

Some people may argue that the quest for meaning is a by-product of the self-indulgence of privilege, as so many work to survive and maintain, pay bills, rent, food, and medical costs. For so many the looming insecurity of retirement without a financial cushion is daunting and purpose is not a consideration; survival is. Shame on me and my precious vanity.

I worry about money all the time. I understand my privilege, but I also know that I am for hire. Retired from teaching and now emerita faculty, I do different contract gigs—interesting work, yes—pay my own health insurance (preexisting condition of cancer, thank you) and a mortgage compounded by property taxes. Health emergencies arise, a roof needs to be replaced.

For now, I am lucky to have regular employment contracts, coaching and editing clients, freelance writing, and speaking opportunities to make one full-time job. And I deeply acknowledge that someone half my age or even ten years younger would be a cheaper hire because I have been told as much. I know I am replaceable. No one owes me their loyalty or my next paycheck.

I also worry about the worth of what I spend my days doing. Whether it matters beyond the moment. To anyone. I worry if I am working hard enough, reaching into enough different arenas, exhausting possibilities. Being kind enough to others. Changing any little thing. Sometimes I have glimpses that the work I do is good, that it is valued; that I am valued. I hope what I contribute to the world matters. Or does it?

And then I measure it in dollars, and I think maybe not. Sure, if I were in some other line of work, I would be more comfortable financially—a lawyer, doctor, start-up genius, public relations consultant? I know I could never have survived in a world of tech or sales or entrepreneurship; I do not like the risk factors, nor I am equipped or knowledgeable enough to succeed in those fields. There are few millionaire professors. Not so many wealthy journalists. Yes, some authors make it very big. Most don't. I don't know how to do much else.

I like to tell stories of all forms. The words move me. I keep doing it because it is what I know how to do. I worry all the time about my income and what I need to keep going, what emergencies may arise, what son may need my help.

Some people I know are not dogged by these concerns. They are not bothered by the mundaneness of tomorrow or next week or next year. A lot of those people have spouses who work and shoulder the bills. Some put these tangible concerns aside. And they concentrate on the bigger picture; I imagine some are blessed with the contentment of their accomplishments as well as their limits of possibilities. I think those people must have healthy 401K accounts. At least I imagine those are the people who are able to sleep on the train as they commute home from work. Aha! They have achieved self-actualization.

Author and Harvard psychologist Shawn Anchor writes that scientists define happiness as a triumvirate of levels: pleasure, engagement, and meaning. The latter aligns with Aristotle's definition for *eudamonia,* or human flourishing. Anchor writes, "This definition resonates with me because it acknowledges that happiness is not all about yellow smiley faces and rainbows. For me, happiness is the joy we feel striving after our potential."

Not that purpose will make you delirious, pay your mortgage or your prescription refills, but I have found that as a writer and editor engaging in many types of work, I am happier when I am working on projects I feel matter beyond the immediate. When what I do and engage in means more than what I can witness in front of me. That is my calming influence. This idea, or ideal, can keep the demons of money worries at bay. For a bit.

The older I get, the more natural it is that there are more funerals I attend, more appropriate flowers I send, more texts I write with closed-prayer-hands emojis and more Facebook comments I post saying I am sorry for your loss. Lately the fallen friends, fathers, mothers, lovers, spouses, mentors, even icons I don't know personally are around my age, some younger, some older.

I am always doing the math.

In doing so, I am trying to inject urgency into the meaning of my work, how I spend the days of my life I have remaining—not that I have a scorecard or a definite expiration date. I admit

I lack the incandescent faith both my mother and father possessed in their lives and deaths, rudders intact, aiming for what they always imagined to be a happy ending. Both of my late parents—devout Catholics for life—knew where they were going all along.

The devoutly faithful have "cognitive flexibility," I understand, and like prolific author C. S. Lewis see the paradox of discomfort and pain not as punishment but as a chance for a growth spurt in faith and a peaceful resignation that in the end, all will be revealed, like the winner in *The Great British Baking Show*.

A recent study as part of the Wellbeing Project that began in 2018 and runs until 2023, focused on genetic contributions to a person's sense of well-being and whether that well-being was hedonistic (associated with happiness) or eudaimonic (associated with the meaning of life). The results from 220,000 DNA samples show a genetic correlation between the types of participants' responses. Some people are wired to find meaning in their lives. That predilection may also help us along the way. Scientists agree that we age better and have fewer physical difficulties if we find purpose.

I am afraid of roller coasters, trolls, texting drivers, violent movies, and the two white pit bulls on Greenfield Avenue who jump and bark ferociously, banging against the fence when I walk past. And I am afraid of not having enough money when I am older, though Colin has told me I can live with him when I am really old.

"What if your wife doesn't like me?" I ask him.

"Well, then she wouldn't be my wife."

I worry about what will happen when no one is asking me anymore to send in eight hundred words on what I think. When editors stop returning emails promptly. I am simultaneously afraid of dying without having an impact. I am afraid that I have not done enough for other people. That the goal of serving others has only been when convenient, even as I schedule a meeting for one of the five boards of advisors where I volunteer.

I could glance at my résumé filled with years of titles and hyperlinks, or a small stack of published books with my name on the cover and the spine. I can look at the photos in my home of my three grown sons—doing well—whose lives depended on me. I can make a rapid mental inventory of people I have mentored, influenced, helped, I hope. But is it enough? Am I enough—ever? I wonder if a bell rings or a certificate arrives, and if you ever really know.

And then come the money worries, burping into view, arriving as reliably as dusk. I am not someone who takes elaborate vacations—if any—nor do I do more than occasionally splurge on impractical shirts at Ann Taylor Loft, using my email coupons. The retirement plan commercials scare me. And they air often.

Feeling as if I may not have accomplished enough is embedded in the feeling that I am not enough. When will I ever be enough? And what is enough anyway? Who decides?

I am not alone in that as a woman. I know for sure I am not alone in that as an older woman. For goodness sake, Viola Davis—winner of an Oscar, an Emmy, and two Tonys—says she has imposter syndrome.

I know I do not have the capacity, intellect, genius, or skill set to change the world on a big scale. But I still want to influence a small piece of it with the work that I can do—however briefly— with the talents I can muster, to be a conduit for others whom I mentor to make their own dent of impact, while pushing myself to do all I can.

I have to know this is not all there is. I cannot bear the uncertainty of the question.

CONNECT

I WAS IN MY LATE FORTIES. STANDING IN FRONT OF A CLASSROOM of about fifty undergraduates in journalism at Northwestern University, as a senior lecturer. I was delivering the final writing prompt of the morning class, 201–1: Editing and Writing the News, a course I created for freshmen journalism majors and a few sophomore transfer hopefuls.

A "weed-out" class, it was called under breaths, tough on purpose, a holdover from the days when I was in school and the professors—all white, mostly men—would lock you out of a four-hour class if you were late, even by a few minutes. No makeups. Good deadline training.

"It's the ten o'clock news, not the 10:05 news," Professor Dick Hainey would say.

I had already been lecturing, asking questions for an hour and ten minutes. At 10:10, with just ten minutes to go, I asked the students to write down a description of me that morning, then leave it on the desk at the front, their name attached. And I left the room.

A few minutes later, as the students, chatting and rumbling, filed out the door on the second floor and headed for the staircases in Fisk Hall, I returned and gathered the sheets of paper with scrawled sentences in blue, black, and red ink, some pencil.

"Professor Weldon is wearing red pants and a black shirt."

I was wearing a blue dress.

"Professor Weldon has an old lady look to her, I gather these are age spots on her face, hands and neck. She is wearing something she shouldn't and appears to be aging gracelessly."

These were not graded assignments. It was a journalism exercise in keenly paying attention, observing, and taking good notes. Find the truth, say what you see, accurately. I assume they interpreted it as an exercise in bluntness. They were to learn how to look, describe, and put into words what they saw. Notice everything. Pretend you are describing the scene to someone who would never be in that room, never bear witness. (In subsequent quarters, I learned my lesson and assuaged my fragile ego by asking the students to describe each other.)

Inaccurate clothing aside, I did not recognize the person they described. It was someone else. I thought then that my age was not the first thing to notice about me. I don't know what I assumed it was—my wit, my charm, my competence?

I guess I was as wrong then as I am wrong now.

I LOOK FOR THE TRUTH IN WHAT I DO AND IN THE TRUTH OF how I am to the world and try to determine whether my perceptions of who I am and what I offer are the same. Trying to connect value for what I do to others, someone, anyone. It is not as easy as it seems. At least not for me.

I discover that I am having more of those moments of isolation where I do not recognize who I am, even bear a passing familiarity with the person whose skin I wear, whose name I own, whose identity is in my wallet. I am watching myself perform a foreign choreography from the back of an auditorium. Squinting to see who she is across the aisle, across the street, across the chasm of another time. Does anyone else feel they are renters in the wrong Airbnb?

Hoping to be authentic. Not obsolete. Praying that what consumes my days and months and years bears some hint of truth, some modicum of a connection of worth for someone. A connection beyond myself. And that when I disappear, at least a footprint remains. The megalomania of it all is dizzying. I know the price of ego, of vanity, and it is not pretty.

But is it unusual to imagine your disappearance and to feel it is already in place?

I have read and heard from far too many who write and talk, talk, talk about the shock of the sudden aging of their children, asking questions on Facebook and Instagram about how did my son so quickly get to be this tall, slender adult, or how did my daughter grow into this mother herself? Where has the time gone?

I never say or write those things because I have never felt that way—that any of this growth or passage for them was sudden, I mean, that my sons were instantly men. I witnessed firsthand the growth and kept tabs on their progress, knowing they were changing, so that the shifting and metamorphosis I was witnessing were not just anticipated, but expected, embraced, welcomed. I was pleased for them to ascend into their own shapes, their own futures, their own lives, fully, independent. I was not caught unaware by their inevitable shape-shifting, I was only surprised to see the shapes that they became. Because, really, wasn't that the whole point? I feel connected to them. It did not happen quickly.

It is me I missed. It's my sudden entry into old age that surprised me. How could it be that I was prepared for my sons to grow old but that I was caught off guard on the same process for me?

MY WRITING DESK FACES THE WALL IN THE FIRST-FLOOR OFFICE that my sons still call the family room, though this has been my daily home office for five years. When Brendan visits from Columbus, where he lives and works, he lies on the couch watching videos on his phone, without headphones, oblivious that I am at my desk typing, writing on deadline.

"I'm working," I say to him, and he always acts as though he is completely surprised, as if I am telling him, "This has all been a dream."

The large picture window facing west looks out into the backyard, my yard, our yard. I pay to have the grass cut, though I trim the bushes. It is utterly fulfilling to plug in a trimmer—mine is red with a succession of very, very long extension cords plugged into the outlet in the garage—and to tame an overgrown and uncooperative wall of bushes, retake control of the yard and see the balding impact, the whirring playing over and over in my ears. It takes several hours three times over the summer to trim all the bushes, and the trimmings can fill up to eight leaf bags that I fold and leave by the street for pickup on Tuesdays.

Today it is snow quieted and still; I can count thirteen houses without craning my neck, all of us paying high property taxes, but it is worth it for the safety, the quiet, and the schools, I told myself and tell myself still, though no one goes to school from this address anymore.

I see the well-kept garages and tuckpointed facades of my neighbors to either side; a house for sale to the north that my friend Anne says is overpriced but they do not need to sell it; the loud neighbors to the east with the pool that my sons used to dive into by sneaking through the back fence. Those neighbors don't like me much, I gather because of the boys diving in their pool with their friends. They called the police about 7:00 p.m. for a high school graduation party in our yard one June, the police saying they had a report there was underage drinking. There was not; I offered the officers a plate of fried chicken. They did not take it but smiled, saying we were warned.

The newer neighbors to the east shoot off fireworks for hours and hours on the fourth of July, many of them landing in my driveway, on top of the garage and on the lawn; I worry that the bushes will catch fire.

The row of bushes to the south include a few hydrangeas, lilac bushes the height of trees, and a stretch of about a dozen clumps of daylilies that each year grow thicker and wider and need to be weeded more often. They are brown and spare now in winter, but in season they offer me bouquets that make me happier than they likely should; my own bounty, cornucopia, growing of its own accord, wildly, madly, without intervention, unless you count the evening watering from the hundred-foot-long green hose with only two holes where water spurts forth.

A cardinal sits on the telephone wire stretched between the pole two backyards away and my yard; I tell myself it is my late father coming to say hello.

I don't know who it is who told me my father came back as a cardinal after he died in 1988, but I have since found that millions of people believe in this mythology—not of my father, but that they are visited by cardinals as a symbol of one who has died, visiting like angels, red and welcoming and deliberate. All of us hoodwinked, calling out to a random red bird by name.

"Hi, Dad," I say aloud.

My mother is supposedly a butterfly; my sisters and I gift each other items with butterflies on them, not all the time, just once in a while, place mats, dishes, pins, knickknacks that my sons will no doubt throw away when I die, not knowing at all it was Mama Pat, their grandmother, and acting as if they have never heard of it before. I bought a butterfly-themed purse last year, excited about it, but it does not have the proper long strap so I can wear it across by chest and walk freely, arms swinging, so I never use it.

I face the wall, not the windows because I don't need the distraction, and I type, write, and edit all day without a sense of myself, just writing, editing, changing, shifting, sending, opening, deleting, saving, typing, editing, saving, sending, opening, deleting.

Unless I have a scheduled appearance on Zoom when I still manage to send texts and emails while pretending to pay attention, or interview sources on the phone for columns and stories, the sounds of my day are the tapping of my fingers on the Lenovo keyboard, the arrival of messages and the sending of photos, a whoosh that is fabricated and absurd, as if we need an aural reminder that something is actually traveling. Moving somewhere, not static, trapped.

Publish. Send. Agree with the edits. Say thank you.

And some days I am in other cities leading a seminar in a room of twenty or more doctors, nurses, lawyers, academics, social justice advocates, all of them yearning to express their ideas in a larger space beyond the silos. Change the world, tell the truth, project urgent ideas that matter to a world embracing the insight.

It is humbling work, uplifting and confronting, what I do for the OpEd Project. Each session I learn how much I do not know about most everything—anthropology, transgender injustice, violence, bias, organ transplants, pediatric emergencies, water shortages, sixteenth-century literature. The depth of commitment many participants have is contagious. So many hunger to tell the truth, to connect. I want to have a professional life connected to truth.

I want what I do to matter. I want the truth to matter. I also want to feel connected and not to feel so separated, so separate. Useless. A former journalist friend—the former is on the friend; she is still a journalist—told me years ago I write about nothing. Maybe I do.

WHEN I WAS GROWING UP IN THE HOUSE ON JACKSON AVENUE, I played jacks alone in the front hall because the marble foyer was smooth and cool and my superball—blue, yellow, red and paint spattered by design—flew higher than my head when I bounced it to pick up my colored shiny jacks as I sat cross legged, concentrating.

No one came in the front door unless they were company—company that was expected—so sitting near the door between that and at the foot of the front stairs, I was not obstructing anyone's comings and goings. We all went up and down the back stairs because those led right to the kitchen, and we could slide through the kitchen past the center island where Mom defrosted the meat for dinner and run out the back door if we didn't want to be noticed (not me: I wanted to be noticed).

Younger than my three sisters, who grew impatient with me and my questions, not a boy like my brothers, who didn't need me or want me for a team or a game of horse with their friends playing basketball in the driveway, I often played alone.

I could concentrate on the jacks, I could talk to myself, I could talk to my imaginary friend Betty Sally, who died suddenly when I turned ten, more a fading than any kind of violent death that would be predictive of more worrisome emotional problems later in life. Her passing was noticed only by my mother, who one day asked about her and I responded that yes, she had died. It was uncharacteristic of me not to have an elaborate backstory—I did think about a kidnapping—but I decided just to say she died as if she had moved on neatly and without a fuss, as though she had boarded a train and it slid away to another state, maybe Nebraska or Montana.

Alone is different than other, and my feeling as other may have been self-imposed, as I could have certainly tagged along with my brothers if I dared, and my sisters would tolerate me, and Madeleine would even agree to play dolls if she was in the mood. But when she was thirteen and I was nine it was an unfathomable distance I did not fully understand, and so I filled my time with jacks, books, and Barbies with the one Ken who lost both his arms, I am not sure exactly how, and conversations with Betty Sally—that is, until she died.

IN MY HOME OFFICE, THE HISSING OF THE RADIATOR AT MY feet and the tapping of my fingers on the keys, those are the songs of the day. I do not answer the house phone ringing upstairs, it is always "Unknown" on caller ID, but I do not stop paying for a landline because I do not know how I would find my cell phone without it. Even the app to locate your phone is *on the phone*—who thought of that?

Sometimes I feel it doesn't matter who I am in the daytime: I can be anyone really, I am someone who does the work, who meets the deadlines, who imagines and arranges and creates and fulfills content requirements and back-and-forths with clients and it is all silent. I could be anybody—not even me—just checking off the boxes in Asana or Slack or ActiveCampaign, filling out a Google form, as required, task complete. Occasionally someone will send a kind note, allude to the possibility that I am real. Otherwise I am an avatar.

When I am out and about and mingling as I am required to do at the work gatherings, the board meetings, the workshops, the seminars, the birthday parties and dinners I attend because Evite and Paperless Post told me I must, I am struggling to stay connected to what I do and to feel validated. Watching myself, listening to the answers that spring forth from my chest, passing through my open lips, and looking into the eyes of my conversation partner who may be reading my name tag or reading my mind.

Sometimes I think about the lipstick I am wearing as I speak and wonder whether it looks like it did on the blown-up photograph at Ulta, and whether twenty-two dollars is really worth it for long-lasting luster, and then I think no, the drugstore kind is better even if it doesn't last as long on my lips or in my purse. I do try to push myself back into my mind and into my body and stay with the focus and the game plan.

This is just what happens: you change over time and you do look and act and sound and smell differently, and it is so gradual it is sudden, but if there were a time-lapse video of your life, you would see. Like the shrinking of the glaciers, the disappearance of the Arctic, it was going to happen and it was going to go away. Just as I am.

I read somewhere that Oscar Wilde said on his deathbed, "These drapes are killing me," and it makes me laugh out loud every time. I tell my sons I want them to play Gloria Gaynor's "I Will Survive" on loop at my wake, but I am only half-kidding, and how would I know if they did or not.

10

SWAP

SHERYL SANDBERG ADMITTED THE AMBIGUITY OF LEANING IN, six years after *Lean In* was published, in a 2019 interview with *Black Enterprise* magazine. "One of the good things about the title *Lean In* is it's a very strong title. And everyone thinks they know what it means. One of the bad things about the title *Lean In* is it's a very strong title—and everyone thinks they know what it means."

What I thought it meant when it was a newish concept was that it's my fault if my ambition doesn't prove strong enough to land me where I want to be, even when I followed all the steps. Because it didn't. I see and hear a lot of women in a lot of TED Talks and self-help podcasts proclaim that vision boards can decide your future, just make it happen! And then I think, perhaps these women aren't paying all their bills with a rosy intention and surely if they can just envision something and it happens magically, then they definitely must have family taking care of their children for free as a favor. Because you can't just perform a simple gesture and make your professional and personal lives the stuff dreams are made of. Or I can't anyway.

Here's a game you can play at home. Raise your right hand if you have a family—a spouse, children, partner. Raise your left hand if you care for parents—in or out of your home. Put your right foot in if you or anyone in your family has health concerns. Put your left foot in if you have hobbies you would like to pursue—anything from knitting to swimming, bridge to kayaking. Do the hokeypokey and turn yourself about.

Or fall over.

This is the hokeypokey work-life balance toxic potion my generation and the generations since have been mandated to drink. As if leaning in was not enough, on the other end of the fabrication, Anne Marie Slaughter in an essay in the *Atlantic* in 2012 claimed definitively that women cannot have it all. The CEO of New America, former director of policy planning at the State Department, and mother of two sons, commuted from Washington, D.C., during the week, to her home in Princeton, New Jersey, for the weekend.

Her husband cared for her boys in her absence. After two years, she left the mad dash of Washington to return to her tenured spot at Princeton University, with no regrets and new insights into the fluffy paradise we call "all." Now she's CEO of New America, a think tank. I get it, we must not be able to have it all.

First we are brainwashed to think it is all just a personal choice, tilt your shoulders a little, follow this prescription, and poof! Then we are told it was not true in the first place. Which is it?

The good news is now we have Serena Williams as a role model for getting it all done, who holds her daughter on her lap as she winds down on the stationary bike after a Wimbledon win and then is named athlete of the decade by the Associated Press.

We can have it all in bits and pieces. We can have it all of it, yes, but not all at once. Working, parenting, elder care, every shift assigned to us whether we like it or not—all require the swapping of duties, prioritizing, selecting. Swap. Swap. Win. Swap. Swap. Swap. Maybe win?

I am grateful for many leaders and role models for the insight, instructions, principles, tools, intentions, courses, checklists, and declarations to teach and show by example that everyone can claim their power to navigate the present and the future on their own terms. Because I have learned I can change my path. But I wish there were a clause of forgiveness in this work-life endeavor when for many reasons, you just can't make it go as planned. That it does not happen the way you envisioned. At all. I want someone to tell me definitively how to feel content as is.

So perhaps instead of making a complicated life into a finite pie-slicing contest, we can concentrate not on balancing the dagger knives of work and life but on acknowledging the difficulty of carrying different plates and adopt the attitude that we are not struggling indefinitely but swapping with finesse. And that all of it is scary.

Swap our obligations—not abandon them, just put them on hold. Your teenager needing ten more hours of driving time with you over your need to be a superstar in the office this week. Your ill mother needing you to be with her at the doctor over your swim time at the gym. Your colleague asking you to mentor her over your wanting to go home early.

I have trouble with the semantics of balancing as assigned specifically to women and work. You don't hear so many men pontificating about balancing their lives. Because balancing implies that you are always perilously on the edge. It means there is a judgmental delicate high-wire act you are always performing. Swapping implies that you are faced daily with an abundance of choices. Balance is about risk and failure. The other—swapping—is about possibility and choice.

I understand what it means to do the responsible thing. To keep the job you don't necessarily love, keep taking on work to pay bills. Enjoying the work, dreading some of the tasks and meetings, still making sure to swap what needs to be done at the time with what can wait. The best thing we can do is brace ourselves, move to the future and try to inhabit it now. Alfred North Whitehead wrote, "Ideas don't keep. Something must be done about them."

Of course I know so much of what has happened for me is because of my privilege, where I was born, how I was raised, education I earned, jobs I had, opportunities I had handed to me, opportunities I stretched out into decades. I have had some success because of that automatic life boost, not because I am the only human being who has ever swapped this for that or dreamed big. And I made choices on what to miss and what never to avoid. I have yet to achieve all I dreamed; what haunts me is the likelihood I never will. I wonder if I ever will feel enough.

I do not blame the women who came before me and declared we need to balance. Because I believe most everyone was just trying to rectify a situation drenched in unfairness on so many levels, steeped in misogyny, racism, ableism, and sexism within systems built to exclude. A lot of the framing was flawed, insufficient, and inconsiderate of historically obvious and more subtle and blatant gaps in fair treatment. And what I suggest is flawed.

Sometimes—a lot of times—the historic and prevailing systems in place have no possible entry point for you, and sometimes the people in charge of the table just do not want you sitting there. Whether it is because of your age, skin tone, race, looks, gender, orientation, religion, ability, affiliation, your "big personality" or that you said something once to somebody's sister, or whoever even knows why, you may never get to understand why the table is always filled up. And it is not because you didn't lean in far enough or balance hard enough or try to get a seat. Or did enough self-care; as a working single parent, self-care was washing my face.

I imagine my life as a swap, not as a balancing act of plates that will fall in the air, crash to the ground and cut my fingers. I know I do not have all the answers and that there are questions I cannot fathom, let alone respond to authentically. So I sometimes swap questions for more questions. And cross my fingers.

11

WORK TO DO

I LOOK AT THEM, I ADMIT IT. THE SLIDESHOWS ON THE distracting websites screaming, "You won't believe what these child stars look like now!" And I'm somewhat embarrassed to say that I do look at them to find out the shocking revelation, though I do not do it a lot, maybe once a week. Or I don't know, maybe it's once a day, and not for that long. This is why they call it clickbait.

And yes, it's true, usually I cannot believe any of it. The "after" shots are visual aftermath like the photos of a total home gut or rehab shots of people whose lives have not been lived necessarily pristinely. Mostly these are cautionary tales: This is how you will end up if you are not supercareful, so do the cleanses, stop smoking and drinking, and never eat another egg or slice of bread again. Usually the ad to the right that flashes briskly sells something to combat this variety of downfall. Lately it involves keto. What did you think would happen if you didn't live like a nun or a monk in the twelfth century; I wonder if they had good skin.

I wrote a story once when I was a feature writer at the *Dallas Times Herald* about a community in the Himalayas where supposedly all the residents lived to be about 105. Their secret was that they had no TV, electricity, fast food, or alcohol.

After reading my piece, my editor said, "Maybe they don't really live to 105, it just seems like it."

I HAVE BEEN WORKING FOR FORTY-FIVE YEARS, AND MAYBE will be working for forty-five more, though that would certainly be a very long time and I would be over a hundred. I have been employed on an hourly, monthly, or annual basis since my first job in 1974 at sixteen at the teen clothing store—"boutique" is a big word—on Lake Street in Oak Park with my friends Jean, Olga, and Marcy and a boss who sometimes rubbed our shoulders when he walked past and always stared at our chests when he spoke to us. We ignored him. After all, we were making $1.65 an hour. Cash.

And yes, this was decades before we knew to call it #MeToo. Most every woman I knew had these experiences. Some were not just inconvenient, but criminal, all of it wrong. Our job was to deftly figure out how to avoid the encounters. And warn our women friends.

I worked in retail because I thought working in restaurants would give me the dry heaves at what people left on their plates. I understood there was no tipping in selling jeans, inexpensive tops, and bathing suits, but at least there was no grossing out—that's what we called it.

After one summer at that store, I worked after school and on Saturdays at a now-defunct chain called Madigan Jr's. on North Avenue in Melrose Park, and I earned a commission, I think about 1 percent. But I could really push the earrings and the bracelets and the socks after convincing someone to buy the coat. Our manager was a nerdy type, and he lectured us in the morning before our Saturday shifts about trends. He was particularly intrigued one Saturday about the future of the ombre look. Another summer I worked at the Limited, where the manager called us "Limited Girls," and I told him I didn't really appreciate the title. Because I did not feel limited. He ignored me.

In college I worked on the *Daily Northwestern* starting freshman year and was mortified when the editor in chief told me to stay after dinner service was over in the dorms so I could work on the edits on my story. The newsroom was on the third floor of Norris Center where the cafeteria below served the best, greasiest patty melts. It had taken me about four or five hours to write a five hundred-word story on a new course at Medill, the journalism school, where I was enrolled, and no one would call me back. I finally got a secretary to the dean to give me an answer to my carefully worded, written questions. I was thrilled.

"You quote whoever answers the phone?" the editor in chief bellowed at me. It shall be noted that this editor went on to have an excellent career in international journalism. I did not.

Apparently this was not what a reporter was to do. I muffled my tears and bought Fritos in the vending machine on the way out about 8:00 p.m. Dinner in the dorms was over.

I kept going back to the *Daily* year after year and made it to editor of Midweek, the weekly features section, my junior year, and we got a monthly stipend. It was a calling, but it was also beer and pizza money, and if I didn't spend it all, it was airfare to Florida for spring break, staying at a friend's family's house because hotels were out of the cost question.

It was the first time—OK, editing and producing the *Juvenile Journal* at ten years old was the first time—I was doing work that I wanted to do forever. I loved every afternoon and evening in college being with friends playing journalist. I was being what I thought was authentic even though I didn't call it that because "authentic" was not a buzzword until much later, like in my forties. AUTHENTIC was what the neon sign said at Chinese restaurants where they served chop suey.

Most every journalism professor I had over the course of my undergraduate and graduate career talked about the raison d'être—and the only reason to live—was to be a reporter or (lucky stars!) an editor for the *New York Times*. I did the math. About 150 students in my class year at Medill and the same number of students in the three other years in the school, plus grad students, with an additional ten, twenty, more years of about six hundred students each year told to get a job at the *Times* or you were nothing. Odds are most of us were going to be disappointed. And some of my friends did make it there, to the top, and yes, they were the best of the bunch. And several of my former students are stars there and doing incredible work.

I did not make it there. It's not that I didn't try, but no, never staff. I accept that I am not good enough. I think I am supposed to be ashamed. The pinnacle was declared at a time when journalism was decidedly different, more finite and sustainable, with a handful of legacy sites, print only, for goodness sake. Of course, it is not that way anymore with so many more options for digital journalistic excellence. But I still felt less than; I didn't succeed as I planned. I fell short. I'm a disappointment.

Fresh out of graduate school in 1979, I went to work for a small regional magazine in the suburbs of Chicago by default. I had sent out more than one hundred hand-typed cover letters—I put them on pale green paper to stand out!—and résumés to magazines all over the country. I had a round of interviews with a few magazines in New York.

One of my interviews was at *Glamour* magazine. After a half day of interviews, a typing and copyediting test for what I think was something like an assistant's assistant third assistant's job, the interviewer asked me if I had any questions.

"Yes," I replied. "How do you get people to pose for the Glamour Don't photos?"

For those who don't know what those are, they are supposedly candid shots on the streets of New York of people wearing the wrong thing. Long before there was public shaming on Instagram or Twitter, if you wore pants that were too tight or your coat was out of date, the wrong color with your skirt, the wrong shoes, you could end up forever memorialized as a "Glamour Don't"—and without a black box across your eyes to disguise your identity. It was the institutional embodiment of snotty mean girl judgment that I endured in grade school and junior high.

"We use staffers for those."

Now I was even more mortified.

"Why would anyone work here?" I asked. I gathered if you showed up wearing the wrong thing, you'd get called in by a photographer to be forever humiliated in the archives of ill-dressed, fashionably clueless Glamour Don'ts.

She didn't answer me. The interviewer may or may not have been accurate; I never found out. I believe she said the job was for a salary of $9,000 a year. Yes, it was 1979, not 1779.

"How can anyone live on that?"

"You need several roommates." She paused. "And some have trust funds."

I had neither. So I took a job in the Chicago suburbs as managing editor of a local glossy monthly magazine, for $15,000. Perfect, I thought; after all, I was a magazine major when your specific major mattered. Not the *New York Times*, but OK. For now.

This magazine—now folded—featured soft news about restaurants and local celebrities and yes, the editor did say I needed to write about the advertisers, but I pretended that wasn't an ethical breach. I was living at home in my parents' house on Ashland Avenue because I was saving to move into an apartment with Mariann on Fullerton Parkway, and it took me two hours to get to work by two trains: one train east into downtown, the second from there up north.

The office on the second floor of a brick walk-up near a Jewel grocery store on Green Bay Road consisted of the publisher, his wife, a secretary, and me. Yet the masthead was filled with other names and job titles, making this look like way more people worked there.

"When is the assistant editor coming in?" I asked about two weeks into the job.

There is no assistant editor, the secretary told me, the name is made up, as are the other positions and surnames, making the operation look much larger than it is.

One late afternoon the publisher came up to me at my desk—something he rarely did, preferring instead to call me into his office.

"Are those new glasses?" he asked.

"Why, no, I have had these glasses a few years."

"Then it's time to get your eyes checked and get a new prescription because you missed three errors copyediting this edition," he scowled, and then walked back into his office and slammed the door.

Six months into the job, the editor said he was "replacing me with a man" and was now changing my position to contributing editor.

Yes, in 1980 it was ten years after forty-six women sued *Newsweek* for gender discrimination. But this was no *Newsweek*, not even close, and there were not forty-six of me, even if the masthead hinted there might be. I did get a month's pay and got another job quickly, one that was downtown by one train, not two. I worked at *ADWEEK* as an associate editor and wrote about fast food, retail, and beer—personal interests at the time. I was twenty-two and moved into the apartment on Fullerton.

A year or so later I went to work at Fairchild Publications out of the Chicago office as a market editor for three years for a marvelous boss; Nancy and I are still friends. Then I headed to Dallas as a feature writer before moving back to Chicago.

I married, had three children, and then divorced. During that time, I wrote a weekly freelance column for several years for the *Chicago Tribune*, worked to piece together freelance contracts, and started teaching in 1996 at Northwestern, my alma mater, until I retired from teaching almost two decades later.

While teaching, in 2011, I began working part of my time for the OpEd Project, continuing writing books and commentary and later starting as editorial director for a women's leadership organization. I fit together disparate Lego pieces of my work to construct a full-time-plus career. It's harder to explain it briefly at parties—and reunions.

I do go to the Northwestern reunions every five years because, well, why not, I'm local and there will be wine and small bites that are usually delicious—mini chicken tacos, vegetable skewers, mini beef sliders, that kind of thing. I just have to be careful with the seafood because I am allergic and going into anaphylaxis would probably make the alumni newsletter.

Dana came in for the fortieth reunion even though she had not set foot on campus since we graduated in 1979 when she drove west to Los Angeles in her beige Chevette she nicknamed "Lord Mushy" because it looked like a mushroom, not because it was emotional.

Wearing outfits we had discussed multiple times, and that Dana suggested I revise from my earlier plan (the coat was too boxy, I looked like I was wearing a raincoat, and the shoes would hurt), we alighted upon the new visitor center on the south entrance to campus that when we went here as students was a concrete walk leading to grass and mud leading to the beach.

What I noticed aside from the fact that my first kiss new student week was there, along with many, many whose faces did not look familiar and whose name tags rang no bells, was that for those of us who had kept in touch—my *Daily Northwestern* friends, dancing partners, and other roommates—was that the frenzied "look at me, ask me how important I am" hysteria had dissipated from earlier reunions.

Yes, the superfamous journalism and theater major megastars who are household names in lots of households were there, but unlike all the reunion years before that I had attended—with everyone clamoring to chatter on about their titles and their homes and their books and their legal cases and their companies and yes, their fame and fortune, and many times their fancy children in fancy schools—it was way more chill. Maybe because at this age, we are happy to be alive?

I guess the most successful ones are retired, living in Palm Springs or Tucson or Naples, and no one is taking inventory of mistakes, or even the accomplishments. For one delicious evening, "How are you?" meant how are you now, how are you feeling, not what is on your résumé. And that, I must say, is different and glorious and a welcome relief. That was the best part of the reunion, that and the photo booth.

The DJ sucked, and even though they played "We Are Family," which I got to dance to with Dana and Laney who was our roommate senior year in the house on Sherman Avenue where we had parties and played that song relentlessly, no one really danced at the reunion. I think the DJ had been instructed to keep the music not so loud so people could talk and hear one another, but I would have loved to dance way more. What a waste.

Common sense dictates I am in the final laps of my professional output, the marathon that started more than four decades ago when I was convinced the universe was all possibility, that I was all possibility. That I could actually achieve what I dreamed of achieving, that it just took time. Time is running out. I have not done what I planned for myself. I didn't make it big.

I work because I want to, I work because I need to, I work because I really don't know what else I would do with my time. Retirement sounds dreadful to me, and I am afraid that I would never put on pants that zip or straighten my hair, and I would do nothing but lie in bed, watch PBS, and yell at the TV when the news comes on. I always feel I have another book, five or ten more in me, that I have more to say, more to learn, more people to interview, and that I have more to write, but who knows if anyone wants to read it. This is the after part of the slideshow, the before is long past. I am still trying to convince myself it is enough. That I am enough.

I wonder if I can forgive myself for not reaching my dreams.

LEAVING TOWN SUNDAY MORNING, DANA AND I WALKED PAST the Hotel Orrington—this is not where we stayed, as it was booked up when I tried to register—across the street from the Northwestern Apartments where we lived our freshman year in 1975. We were eager to reenact a photo of us standing there fall quarter, clueless, arms around each other's waists. Bursting with tomorrows.

We walked near the valet parking stand where the head valet recognized me; I park there when I have attended events for the Public Voices Fellowships over the last eight years, though I had not been there in months.

"I know you," he smiled. "Nissan."

I misheard him, thinking he said, "Lisa." I smiled back, "I'm Michele."

"No, Nissan. You have a black Nissan Rogue with all the faculty stickers in the window."

PART THREE

MEANING

12

DREAM

EVERY FALL—OCTOBER, TO BE PRECISE—I THINK I AM GOING TO DIE.
That is, until after my annual mammogram and the kind doctor, who is used to my perhaps irrational fears, tells me it has not returned and that I am fine. I usually leave his office in tears, text my sisters, and sob silently a bit more before treating myself to a stroll through the fancy mall on Michigan Avenue in Chicago where his office is. It has a Bloomingdale's and a Banana Republic as well as White House Black Market, where nearly everything is always on sale, even if none of the slim-hipped pants ever fit.

I am not paranoid, I am not overly negative, and I do describe myself when asked as a glass-half-full kind of personality, though a friend of mine says I am more "the glass is there with something in it" sort of person. A realist, not an optimist. There is a difference.

Aretha Franklin was sixteen years older than me when she died, so it gave me pause, not just that I have not done at all anywhere near a single thing as significant or lasting as the Queen of Soul, but that sixteen years is not as long as the warranty on my furnace. Anthony Bourdain was just a few weeks shy of his fifty-eighth birthday, though I get it that it's more complicated than that, as was the death of Kate Spade, at fifty-five, who died on my birthday. Linda's father, who passed in hospice, was twenty-five years older than me. The ESPN reporter who died suddenly of pneumonia was only three years older than my oldest son. When COVID-19 engorged the globe with its terror, the death rates were astounding and made me think almost daily about the random illogic of catching it and dying from the contagion, the frailty of life and the arrogance of trying to make sense of it all.

Years ago I heard someone on the radio talking about aging, and he described the process of growing older with a metaphor of an automobile. Every car wears out. Every car owner has an expectation—a warranty even—of how long the parts will last; it is a given that this car will not last forever. As you put miles on your car, you will have most definitely replaced some parts as they have inconvenienced you by rusting, wearing out, simply not working anymore. The car will be retired to the junk heap eventually.

Humans are the same. At the time the explanation felt heartless, but now it feels pragmatic. No one gets to defy reality and drive a car—or a body—one million miles. There is no age-defying magic trick. You have as many miles under the hood as you can get. And then you don't get any more. And yes, the make, model, and maintenance schedule matter. As does the climate. And the privilege, resources, and access. Of course.

THE OTHER NIGHT I HAD A DREAM, AND IN IT MY MOTHER WAS about fifty years old, about the age she was when I was sixteen and smoking cigarettes in the shower to mask the smell and tearing the pages out of my history and Latin textbooks to tuck into

my book bag every day at high school so it looked lean and empty; that way none of the boys would think I was smart. I didn't
want to be smart outside of the classroom. I wanted to be liked.

In the dream I was the age I am now, sixty-one. I am sitting in
a beige uncomfortable chair in a crowded doctor's office waiting
area that I do not recognize. There are plenty of doctors' offices
in real life where I have been a regular, and I know the mauve
couches and I know the assistants and I smile and ask them how
their children are. Hoping the answer is that they are OK. This
is not one of those offices.

The funny thing about this office—other than my mother is
in it with me and is younger than me, oh, and that she is alive,
having passed away in 2002—is that there as many patients as
there are dogs. Pretty dogs, long-haired golden retrievers and
tiny snow-haired huskies with wagging tails and leashes held
tightly. Everyone has a dog—or rather, everyone is paired with
a dog. There is no barking, just a clinking of leashes and collars.

A woman—presumably a nurse—comes over to me and puts
a rather large dog in my lap and explains that I will be holding
the dog throughout my treatments. It becomes apparent that I
am there for cancer treatment, as the cancer has returned. That
is, in my dream, I have cancer again, something I had in 2006
and have been free of since.

It is not new for me to dream I have cancer, because every
year I think it has come back. That is because I had the kind of
cancer that comes back, likely that it will. It doesn't feel pessi-
mistic to say that, it feels as if I am not in denial and that I will
not be shocked when I hear the words, though I know I will be
shocked when I hear the words because they are shocking words.

When I read about celebrities who die from cancer or friends
who relapse, my first thought is for them, but my second
thought, thirty seconds later, is that it's gonna be me again, but
it has not been yet. Then I think about all the filed paid bills in
the Tupperware bins upstairs and in the basement, and I think
what a mess it will be for someone to sort through, and then I

think I better clean my closets. And I start to wonder if I should get a Dumpster and just throw away everything I am not using and my sons will never want.

I also flash to my dream of getting to Australia, not necessarily Hawaii, though I have a good friend—former student—there who swears she will host me, and then I hope onward to Thailand before I have no more time. I hear the food is good, even though pad thai is a made-up American dish. The flight is long, but I will wear the compression socks.

In my dream I am sitting with my mother, who is wearing a knit suit and Ferragamo shoes, size 8AA, her legs crossed at the knees, a rather large purse in her lap. The purse is white, a lunch-bucket style that was popular in the 1970s.

I have so many purses from my mother, maybe twenty of them, that were relegated to me by my sisters after she died. I have an orange leather shoulder bag with a gold clasp that many people remark on if and when I wear it. There are alligator purses, not to mention the tan alligator briefcase, and the Judith Lieber bags, the rhinestone minaudières I tote along to weddings and leave on the table because they look so pretty next to the wire basket of fresh rolls, sometimes pumpernickel.

My mother was not afraid to die. She lost my father when he was only sixty-six and she was sixty-five, and the six of us children were grown and long gone from the downsized house on Ashland Avenue with the attached garage and the yellow chintz couches in the basement. She died in hospice at eighty and seemed at peace, calm, accepting.

What my mother was afraid of, I believe, was being silenced while she was alive. So she took every opportunity to say what she believed—and some of it was not always what we wanted to hear. She opined to whomever was within earshot at dinners, family gatherings, public celebrations, fund-raisers, meetings, even my book signings. She once got up and left a bridal shower in the mid-1970s because the couple lived together before the wedding. They called it "living in sin" back then, at least my mother did. She earned an MBA at sixty; she was well read and well informed and was willing to tell you so, even if you did not ask.

I feel sometimes now, looking back, that my mother, born in 1922, the oldest of eight, was shown that women were relegated to the kitchen and the back of every room, without a voice, to serve and raise children in compliance and obedience and that was that. A child of the Great Depression, she looked past her circumstance and the roles demanded of her. She had bigger plans, and in her later years she was chief financial officer at my father's manufacturing company that my brother Paul ran after my father died; Paul is still at the helm.

I have always been outspoken, likely because of her, but I have fears of not being valued for what I say and do. I feel that if I am not always in motion, not always producing, I am invisible, have no worth. And if you feel that way—even if for a moment—you will always die too soon, no matter how old you are. Because you feel it is the doing that matters, not you.

In the dream, the dog I have been assigned in the doctor's office is licking my face and I am squirming, not that I am not a dog person, but I guess I can admit, well, I am not so much a dog person. I like other people's dogs, but I do have a pet allergy and it's not just cats, it's dogs too.

We had two dogs when I was growing up, not at the same time of course. Jet, a mix of many undetermined breeds, and a miniature schnauzer we only had a few days.

Jet bit me on my finger when I was about five and my mother gave it away the next day. I have a long scar on my index finger; I remember it hurt when Jet bet me and it bled quite a bit. She said we could not have a dog in the house who bit me or any of my five brothers and sisters, though my brothers Bill and Paul blamed me for getting bitten and being the cause of Jet's sudden departure.

I got several stitches from Dr. Dwyer, who wore his pants high above his belly. My mother took me to his office for the stitches, but he often made house calls. When more than one of us was sick, my mother was kind of relieved, not that any of us was sick but that it was then a two-for-one house call, kind of like buy one, get one free. Dr. Dwyer moved methodically to each bedroom to tend to the ill sibling, sitting on the edge of the bed, his stethoscope around his thick neck.

I gather in the dream I was receiving chemo—because this is not how my breast cancer was treated in 2006 when I received brachytherapy, or internal radiation, over the course of ten treatments. I was told to sit in a chair and hold this dog on my lap who was rather large and fidgety. The nurse adjusted a tube in my arm and I was not happy.

My mother was in the chair across from me and did not look up from her reading. In the dream I couldn't see what she was reading, but she tended to read national best sellers and topical books, collections of stories too, along with the occasional reread of a Shakespeare favorite.

I was not surprised in the dream that my mother was ignoring me, I was just pleased she was there. It was similar to the feeling I have at times that my late mother is with me, long gone, invisible, but present in a cubicle of my mind, perhaps just a memory of her, a flash, but there all the same.

I asked the nurse to please remove the dog, who was at this point nuzzling my neck.

"This will help you to relax," she insisted. It was part of the therapy, she explained.

"Please get him off me," I insisted.

The nurse hissed at me and told me I was ungrateful. I remember being shocked that she was mean. I had cancer, after all, and wasn't she supposed to be nice to me? Damn your therapy experiment, I thought, and my mother looked at me and didn't say anything. And then I woke up.

When I did, I missed her, reminded of how she might have been, sitting with me through a treatment. She would have remained quiet and calm—that is, until the doctor came in, and then she would have asked a lot of questions. She did come to visit me in the hospital in Chicago after I had an emergency appendectomy in the 1980s, and she did come to visit after each of my sons was born. But mostly I was not sick while she was alive; she was the one who needed care, she was the one in the hospital frequently. She was the one I brought flowers to.

WHEN I WOKE UP I WONDERED IF I DID HAVE CANCER AGAIN and didn't know. And I wondered if my mom knew. Because I think that because she is gone—as is my father—they both know everything.

13

FULL OF YOURSELF

I NEVER FELT INVISIBLE BEFORE AS I DO NOW AT TIMES, NOT AS a child, especially not as a child.

Running to the basement of the house where my mother was doing laundry most all of the time, I did not even ask her if she wanted to listen, just jumped into performing the song I wrote for her on the viola. In fifth grade, I was terrible at the viola. The bow screeched across the strings because I was too impatient to apply the rosin before each practice session. No doubt the song was intolerable as well; she never said as much.

I wanted her to hear me. To see me. She did.

My viola playing was not just a little bit not so good but nails-on-a-chalkboard torturous because I never held the bow the way the instructor showed me to or used the right amount of pressure to elicit the smooth melody, but my mother never told me that. And I never believed I was really bad at anything, which can be a curse when you're growing up. You have this bubble around you that you think will protect you from the world, but it won't, not really. You find out eventually.

It wasn't that my parents gorged us with a false sense of bravado about everything, but they did oblige us all with acknowledgments regularly and praise, lots and lots of praise. Favorite dinners for excellent report cards, hugs and rewards from the small dessert to the larger permission to do something longed for—like a horseback riding class an hour away.

My father's nickname for me in first grade was "VG," for "Very Good," which is what I got on my report cards, the early ones that didn't bear grades.

I was born in the generation before they gave out trophies to preschoolers for showing up at soccer practice. My parents were conjoined in pumping each of us up, with the expectation that we would succeed; never punishing us severely for failures but always positively reassuring that it will just take time and practice. We were rewarded for trying. I never got better at the viola. I never got better at swimming or any other sport, I just moved on to other things, I guess when I realized I was not very good. Actually, when I realized I was very bad.

You eventually understand that what your parents adore in you is specifically why people think you are full of yourself.

"You are so full of yourself, Michele Weldon," a girl with freckles and a mean streak said to me the summer of 1964 when I was six.

We were standing by the concrete side of the Riverside swimming pool one July afternoon and I was going on and on about how I would be a famous writer one day after I had reached my peak as a famous ballerina. I was wearing my bright blue swimsuit, dipping my toe in the water with a swish and a splash, putting on my bathing cap with a snap.

She squinted at me in disdain, waiting for my response.

I stayed silent, wondering why would she be so mean. I had never been mean to her.

She stormed off when I didn't cry or react the way she

thought I would, I guess with an apology and an eruption of tears. But I just stared at her, thoroughly perplexed, wondering why she would say such a thing. Susan didn't talk to me the rest of that afternoon nor the rest of the summer nor the five summers after that. It was awkward and it did make me feel bad after all, but I never let on to her.

I asked my mom about it later that night, after the dishwasher was turned on following dinner and everyone had disappeared to their rooms or out to the backyard for the last gasps of a summer night.

"Well, why would you want to be empty of yourself?" my mother asked.

Now, that made sense. You want to be full, like a lunch box headed to school, like a gas tank before a road trip, like an envelope from a pen pal across the world. I love that line so much, I use it in seminars and used it often in my university classrooms. I am considering painting it on my bedroom wall.

My mother said that a lot. To my brothers, Bill and Paul, and especially to my sisters, Mary Pat, Maureen, and Madeleine, and me, who had our share of mean girls to contend with over the years, the ones who told us we would never be OK.

No one likes you. He doesn't like you. You're not pretty. You're not smart. You're fat. You're weird. Everyone hates you.

"They're just jealous," my mother would say.

How you are perceived is separate from who you are; the reaction to you is out of your control. No, you should not be a braggart, a brat, self-conscious—that's a sin. But if you are doing what you enjoy, harming no one else, you are not responsible for how people take you. That, I later discovered, is not how most people my age were raised.

Pre–social media, a lot of the verbal judgment and cruelty thrown at me was about what I looked like. Spared so much cruel harassment as a white, cis, and able-bodied female, I was mocked for what I wore. Most everyone was. If you wore the wrong thing, accidentally, thinking that a pink sweater vest was the coolest thing in the world, only to find out that pink sweater vests were dorky, or that if you did not have the right winter coat or brand of hat or if your pants were not tight enough or low enough, then you were nothing. Nothing. This is why Glamour Don'ts resonated.

But it was one moment that passed and not one that lived forever digitally or went viral.

If you wore something too short, too tight, too flashy, too baggy, too old, too uncool, then you were dismissed, taunted. What you put on your body bred acceptance.

My mother would have none of that: You wear what you like. You be who you are.

If I came home from school and repeated a mean comment, my mother would say, "It's like a dog barking at you. Would you cry if a dog barked at you?"

"Don't let it get to you, Mich," my father would say in shorthand.

At home, I felt seen. I felt loved—even in my teen years when I was sneaky and they didn't see me when I sometimes poured vodka from the liquor cabinet into a cough medicine bottle that I had emptied into the bathroom sink to bring to high school dances and share hurriedly with a half dozen friends outside the school. I knew it wouldn't be OK if my parents knew what I was doing—drinking or hiding cigarettes in my socks. But I also knew that I could teeter off toward the edge because I was tethered and I would not get lost. Or fall off. They would see me.

And I know now I am incredibly fortunate that nothing traumatic ever came from any of my daring. I was not harmed. I was lucky to be unscathed—so many other girls like me were not.

I wanted to be noticed. I wanted my parents to notice me. I wanted my brothers and sisters to notice me. I wanted girlfriends to notice me to invite me over to play at their houses so we could dance in the basement to 45s on the record player. Later I wanted boys to notice me, to like me, to hold my hand, to tell me I was pretty, to call me on the yellow house phone in the kitchen.

I did not want to be forgotten. I wanted to be known for something, something that was mine. It was not the viola, as it turned out. It was not any sport. It was not singing or dancing, even though I took lessons, or math.

It was writing.

It's why I wrote poems and gave them to my parents. It's why I entered contests for writing. It's why I tried so hard, and when I won, my mother would say, "Of course you did!"

It's why the whole family and my fifth-grade teacher, Miss Daus, went to the Palmer House for the 1968 Father of the Year awards dinner because I wrote an essay about how my father was so simple and kind and was one of ten finalists. It's why years later, my father kept all the newspaper clippings from my articles in the college newspaper, then later the ones in newspapers and magazines, in a drawer by his bed.

Once when I was home visiting after college, he was lying on his bed in his blue pajamas in their bedroom with the blue and silver wallpaper, reading a magazine with one of my bylined stories in it. He looked up, and all I could see were his big black framed glasses and the biggest smile.

"This is really something, Mich."

I hear him saying that in my head still.

14

PRIVILEGE

"I WISH I WAS BLACK."

I was thirteen years old in 1971, a freshman in high school, when I declared my wish to my father after watching another Saturday afternoon broadcast of *Soul Train* on channel 26 in the family room of our five-bedroom house in River Forest, Illinois.

I thought the difference between Black and white was the music.

Watching the show from the *L*-shaped leather couch, what I wanted more than anything was to be able to move like *that*. And be a part of the music that sounded like *that*. It was really not much of a musical choice now, was it? Paul Revere and the Raiders, the Carpenters, and the Monkees compared to Aretha, Diana, Gladys Knight and the Pips. I wanted to wear clothes like *that*, tight and smooth and in bright colors, all flowing down the *Soul Train* line; they all looked so confident and cool.

This was not *American Bandstand*. Don Cornelius was not Dick Clark. The girls and boys on *Bandstand* looked serious and crisp and stuck-up and not anywhere near as uninhibited as the *Soul Train* dancers. On *Bandstand*, I didn't like the boys' haircuts and the stiff curls on the women who looked rehearsed and self-conscious.

My father paused. "They don't have it so great."

I didn't ask any questions.

Later I sent away for *The Greatest 64 Motown Original Hits* with cash in an envelope to a P.O. box number I copied down from the commercial. It took me weeks to save the money for the four-record set. I played it so much that I knew the words to every Marvin Gaye and Tammi Terrell song by heart.

Smokey Robinson, the Jackson 5, the Supremes; oh, I didn't blame Diana Ross for leaving: she was clearly more talented and meant for bigger things. I loved how brave she was to go off on her own. She was glamorous and thin. All the TV commercials for exercise machines and ropes you could hang on your doorknob to pull so you could be thin and pretty featured white women looking for fitness. I thought Diahann Carroll on *Julia* was gorgeous.

I didn't have a hint I was privileged; most cocooned white children don't. The news stories on TV, on the radio, and in the *Chicago Tribune* and *Chicago Daily News* that both arrived at our house every day seemed so distant and unrelated to me. I read the comics—*Brenda Starr*—and the food pages for recipes, plus the horoscopes, not the news or business stories for sure. Most everyone I saw represented was white.

Saying you were "out of" something meant all you needed to do was go to the basement wall of shelves for a refill of canned green beans, baked beans, or early June peas, or the freezer in the basement that was filled with steaks, ground beef, pork chops, and chicken breasts. Or the pantry filled with pretzels, Bugles, and cupcakes from Kay's Bakery. We were never really out of anything.

In her 2018 book *White Fragility: Why It's So Hard for White People to Talk about Racism*, sociologist author Robin DiAngelo says "pillars of whiteness" can "trigger a range of defensive responses." Mostly this is because white progressives—I would put myself there—belong to a system of racism "into which I was socialized." DiAngelo adds, "The racial status quo is comfortable for white people." I believe so. I own my oblivion.

Wrapped in the safety of a system I automatically benefited from, I did see hints of the nuances of hierarchy. I had gone in sixth, seventh, and eighth grades to the Convent of the Sacred Heart, an all-girls prep school on Sheridan Road on the North Side of Chicago. My class of twelve girls included the daughter of a Japanese diplomat and the daughter of a gadget magnate who had built an empire on simple devices such as the Pocket Fisherman and home barber sets (my classmate was featured in the commercial for the home barber tool, sitting in a barber's chair, a sheet around her like a shroud).

It seemed other girls in my class at Sacred Heart had more money in their purses than I did. My best friend, Catherine, lived on Astor Street, but I didn't really know it was that big a deal. Mostly everyone's father traveled for work, everyone's mother was pretty—or trying real hard to be. One of my classmates, Kathy, saw her mother, Jane Byrne, become mayor of Chicago.

Most of my classmates had summer homes—owned or rented. Summer homes were smaller places, cabins maybe, usually lakeside in Wisconsin or Michigan or Indiana or one of the cluster lakes in Illinois. Sometimes they were in Florida, but those were the winter homes. Some families had ski homes, beach homes, homes in the woods.

I did not realize until I was older that most Americans did not own any home at all.

I'm not proud to say I was this way; I know it is blind, unforgivably ignorant, and that it dawned on me slowly—not in a sudden epiphany—that white privilege created and sustains my circumstances. As a child, I presumed everyone went out to dinner on a whim. My mother talked about eating everything on your plate because of starving children in China but never about the hungry children on the other side of Austin Boulevard, the dividing line between the nearby predominantly white suburb of Oak Park and their predominantly Black neighborhood of Austin Village on Chicago's West Side.

Racist words were not spoken in our house, but I knew they were cruel because of the way people's faces looked when they said them. These were words I might hear from strangers in a store or a movie theater or later in high school. When they landed in the air, they felt spiked, vicious, like poison. I saw that they hurt, wounded the person who was targeted and on whom they landed. I knew never to say those words. I knew to speak up against using the words. My comfort was never at risk.

In high school, conflict over race was simmering under every surface. There was a confrontation one afternoon after school when a Black male student who was in many of my classes was surrounded and threatened by a group of older white boys who were called "greasers," a carryover from the '60s, I guessed. No one was physically hurt, a few were suspended, no large escalation. I knew it was wrong.

All my teachers were white except some of the gym teachers and a math teacher or two. All the administrators were white, most all the security guards and the hall monitors too. Some of the janitors were Black. Gym class was a problem only if there were Black girls on the opposite team of some of the loud bully white girls, who could push and shove and complain about points. But the gym teacher called them out and it was over soon enough.

Throughout nearly all my life, in the spaces I have been, I am in the insulated comfort of the majority—I am regularly in rooms and organizations of mostly white people, even if professionally the rooms are filled with mostly white *men*. Newsrooms were that way, academia as well; they still are: majority white, majority male. In meetings, at conferences, in the everyday transactions of doing my work, both sexism and racism existed, but it was my experience that the women stood up for one another, across racial identities. Although yes, some white women were just mean.

One week I spent in Nairobi, Kenya, giving workshops with two colleagues for the OpEd Project in 2016, I was the only American white woman in any venue I was in, from restaurants to hotel lobbies to stores to conference rooms; the white women I encountered were mostly British. I had a new perspective as an "only." There on business, it went well, so there is no equivalence. I see that. No negative assumptions were assigned to me, at least none that I felt.

What is starkly different—since 2016 in the United States—is that professionally and in random, casual spaces, I am automatically perceived as a bigoted, microaggressive stereotype; some people say as much. It is understandable; racist white people have ruined, if not eliminated, possibilities of trust as they propagate the systems built to ensure inequities that strangle every aspect of daily lives. I experience lately as an older white woman that I am suspect; I am told on social media or in person at parties, conferences, or meetings that women like me are responsible for who was put in the White House and all the racial hatred that has flourished. For the record, I didn't put him there. Still, I get it. The pain racism causes is persistent.

That is a fair aspersion because white supremacy in this country is open; undisguised, unrepentant, ubiquitous. Smiling white men and women marching with signs and flashing hand signals at football games and in Congressional hearings; racists are no longer even pretending to be nonracist. It's as common a practice as chewing gum. Every day a new act of white hate emerges online, and that hate looks like me.

It is not news that racism, antisemitism, and bigotry on U.S. campuses are commonplace; in many workplaces a given; in public places a common threat. It makes sense for Black, brown, Asian, and Native American people, Muslims and Jews, anyone regularly targeted by white rage, to be wary and self-protective against violence, trauma, subtle or overt assaults, and to prepare, to brace for the unprovoked, ubiquitous hate in the systems, in the streets, and in a one-on-one chance encounter. It's fair game to guess that as a white woman I am perceived as the enemy too.

The violence and racial hatred on YouTube and Twitter affirm that bigotry is expressed openly—at the gas station, Starbucks, Burger King, Target, Walmart, in every city and every state. With every unprovoked and outrageous video capturing a racist screed by a white woman —calling the police on any Black person; screeching in a parking lot; yelling violent, vicious, hateful rants from a car window; blocking a father and son from entering an apartment building; refusing to step aside—I feel shame. I am sorry for the pain caused. I speak up.

For every "Go back where you came from" taunt, shove, gunshot, murder, violence to any immigrant or someone assumed to be an immigrant, I feel shame. For every white murderer targeting people in churches, synagogues, or movie theaters, I feel outrage, horror, and shame. And I am sorry. I speak out.

For every anecdote I hear about all-white panels at conferences and about white women treating Black, brown, Asian, Native American, or any people cruelly at work or anywhere, I feel shame. I am sorry. I work to make the panels I am on and the conferences I attend inclusive. I work to be fair and inclusive in my work and my interactions. I speak up.

I am ashamed, because many white individuals make all white people monsters.

None of this is new; and my apologies if it seems absurd and sheltered to state the obvious. For more than a thousand years white people have been complicit, silent, or orchestrating injustice. And even when some progress feels in place, more white people defy history and claim the past is not true: they want to erase the truth; uphold the systems, the foundations, and the statutes; reframe the narrative so they bear no responsibility or consequence. I am ashamed.

The screen shots today of white women raging randomly in public are similar to the photographs of the contorted faces of white women screaming at Elizabeth Eckford, a Black fifteen-year-old, entering Little Rock Central High School in Arkansas in 1957 after the all-white school was ordered to desegregate. The onslaught of hate toward others feels relentless, timeless, endless. The injury racism causes never subsides.

I understand I have no basis for complaint; mine is an observation, and maybe it is just plain foolish to write this or say it out loud; many observers would justifiably say it's about time, that I deserve the automatic distrust. The assignations people have for me certainly are not comparable to the centuries of endured trauma and brutality. I am assumed to be a racist until I can prove otherwise. That is privilege too, to feel race rage aimed at me to be a new experience. I can understand why it is there, so I work to listen, speak out, act, become an ally, not just in what I write but in what I do. I know never to suggest any parallel experience or equivalence. I cannot expect anyone to want to be my ally. Nor can I expect the benefit of the doubt. I must earn it.

WHEN I WAS THIRTEEN, I DIDN'T KNOW HOW EXACTLY I WAS going to be Black, and I didn't know what my father meant in his response. It was not intentional appropriation or reduction to a stereotype; I thought it was innocent appreciation. But I know now it was my bias and I was shallow and ignorant of the despair behind every song. I loved the music—it was better—and I sincerely wanted to be as confident with myself as the dancers seemed to be. I relished every second of that hour on Saturday when at the end, Don Cornelius gestured with his fist, "Peace, love, and soul."

I didn't realize then that everybody wasn't assured from the time they could walk that college would be paid for and of course they would go. And I didn't know it was not true for everyone that you applied for jobs and likely got them, and that the American Dream was real for only a few. I didn't get it that it was not a given that you decide what you want to be when you grow up. I didn't know all the magic was only if you were white and middle class. Or that occasionally some miraculous intervention prompted the reversal of fortunes for some, but that was the exception. This is not a justification for my unknowing. I know now.

I don't have any excuse as an adult for not knowing or pretending privilege doesn't skew everything. It is up to me to learn more, know more, do more, be more, listen more, ask more. That is my privilege—to work to be on the right side of wrong, to earn trust, to see how I can influence a shift, to be worthy of being an ally. It's not enough to be a bystander. It's not enough to say, "Not me." I need to do anything I can to affect change.

The year the Rev. Dr. Martin Luther King Jr. was killed, and Bobby Kennedy too, was the summer of the 1968 riots in Chicago, just an El ride east from our house. The mayor of Chicago was Irish like us, the first Richard Daley, who was loud like my mother's uncles and I didn't think he was so smart. His face was round and red and he talked in clipped sentences in an accent that was nasal and harsh like the Chicago winters and full of dirty salted snow. The evening news had all old white men—except for thirty-eight-year-old white Barbara Walters—sitting at desks talking through their glasses about Vietnam and police brutality.

The April night after Dr. King was shot and it was on the TV news, my family said a prayer for Dr. King and his family in the living room after dinner when we said the Rosary.

"He was a very good man," my father said.

Of course my father could have said more. about history, injustice, racism, and pain—and how privilege exempted us from all of that despair and anguish. Maybe he only wanted to delay what I would later learn was a world that was only accessible to those who are white with the automatic benefit of privilege. Maybe he was hoping it would be a while before I learned that presumptions and bias ruled your past, present, and future. And that it was not fair, and it was firm. I definitely could have learned more, inquired more, demanded more in grade school and high school and college to understand more about everyone in the world with their own proud cultural identities and what it meant, but I didn't. I raised my sons differently.

I know empathy is a muscle you can stretch and fortify. There is no expiration date on learning more, doing more, and being a person who stands for fairness every day.

What I craved when I watched *Soul Train* was what I witnessed as palpable Black joy: men and women seen and heard as they are, genuine in the moment, defined by the best possible perception of themselves. That I was so unforgivably myopic in my views when I should have seen what was in front of me, around me, everywhere, makes me cringe. To see difference only in terms of music is wildly offensive.

I was involuntarily granted white privilege at birth and have reaped a lifetime of allowances and rewards because of it.

I voluntarily use that privilege to influence a difference. The work I do sharing, endorsing, amplifying and listening to the truth telling of every person can hopefully affect real change.

I wish I was better. I am working on it.

15

LAP LANES

AT THE LOCAL PARK DISTRICT POOL, WHERE I COME ALMOST every evening in the summers from 5:30 to 6:00, I am the old lady in the lap lane. I am not the crabby old lady in the lap lane, which is good: I smile and say hello and good-bye to the lifeguards before and after my laps no matter how undeservedly brusque I think they are with me. I hope with every little cheery wave I offer that, in the case of an emergency, it will be the reason they jump in right away to save me and not pause and think to themselves, *Ugh, not her.*

I swim in the same pool where I took my three children when they were young and never seemed to get tired; now I wonder how many laps I have left in me.

My father died at sixty-six—five years older than I am now— taking his last breath at the hospital once my mother went home to shower, following days and weeks at his bedside in a vigil.

Sparing her was his final act of kindness, after a lifetime defined by unbroken gestures of kindness.

I dive in the deep end and abandon the ever-racing thoughts of all my daily business. I cannot, however, successfully annihilate the notion of dying that lately pops up more frequently, especially on the anniversary of my breast cancer diagnosis—stage 1—which was followed by a lumpectomy, brachytherapy, and years of follow-up medications.

Kelly Clarkson is singing on the loudspeakers, echoing around the walls of the main building. This song is old by the standards of the young lifeguards here—2009. I know because I sang it a lot in the car while driving my three sons to practices and wrestling meets: "Because of you, I find it hard to trust not only me, but everyone around me. Because of you, I am afraid."

My mother lived to be eighty. Her last three years were mostly spent in bed at home and then in hospitals; the final months she had a breathing tube, and her last hours were belabored—suffering, gasping.

For me getting old happened suddenly—or maybe I was too busy working or raising children and trying to make a dent in what I thought was my life's larger mission to pay attention to it. No gradual hinting, no inch-by-inch increments, no sliding down the hill once I was over it; old age for me arrived with a slam . . . or maybe with the quiet flipping open of a chart, thirteen years ago, in an oncologist's office.

While I swim, there is a gentleman who arrives at the pool in a rolling walker—the kind with a seat—pushing ahead, his back hunched. At a lounge chair, he deposits his bag on a nearby chair (I imagine it contains a towel and his car keys) and pushes the walker close to the side of the pool. He grabs onto the stairs and, with what looks like great effort and discomfort, angles his body into the water. He swims laps smoothly in a lane near mine; I realize it is perhaps the only time of day when his body complies with his mind's instructions.

My grandmother, when she was alive, used to call the obituaries the "Irish comics," and I thought that was odd because they weren't then and even now aren't funny. But now, I too read them most days. I used to glance at the obits for the parents of friends, and through tears, I have read them for the sons and daughters of loved ones. Now it is my friends, and friends of friends, who are featured—neighbors, coworkers. All of it, for some reason, feels like a shock.

The loudspeakers start booming a song from Adele's first album; I know every song on that CD by heart because I used to sing to it on the long drive to work.

"When did this song come out?" yells the high schoolish boy sitting in the lifeguard's chair to the young woman resting above the lap lanes.

"Two thousand ten," she shouts back, peering up from what I imagine is a necessary and regular close inspection of her split ends.

"Two thousand eight or nine," he corrects her, in a voice louder than a whistle, the one he blows when someone touches the plastic lane divider in alternating circles of azure blue and white. "Wow, that is old."

The song is not old to me; I am old to me.

I used to occupy the office of an older adjunct at the university who was found dead in her apartment from a heart attack after she did not show up to teach a class. The desk drawers I inherited from her were filled with ketchup packets and paper clips.

"I feel creepy being in her office," I told David.

"We're all in offices of dead people," he said. And he was right.

There's a mother-son duo who are here most later afternoons into evenings as well, both lean and with the same length of midback curly brown hair, his in a ponytail. He appears to be in his thirties, about the age of my oldest son, and she seems to be my age. When she sits on the side of the pool in her bikini, calling him "dear," her stomach has thin, crisp folds like a manila envelope.

The water is soft; odd how water can feel buttery. I know it is harming my hair and that I will need to go home and rinse out the chlorine quickly or I will have an unnatural tint on my otherwise L'Oreal No. 9 crown. I don't wear a bathing cap.

Mixed in with the pop tunes are the sounds of children laughing in bathing suits the color of party balloons and their mothers occasionally yelling from the lounges where they squint at their phones—the latest versions—guarding piles of towels defined by superheroes, stripes, florals, or palm trees.

Eyes closed, I float on my back, listening, holding my legs straight out in front of me, toes pointed, arms stretched out in a crucifixion, then swiftly moving my arms deliberately together to the sides of my body, pushing the water to my core, a floating corpse.

I'm doing backstroke—a low-speed, low-key, reverse-on-my-back froggy breaststroke not endorsed by the U.S. Olympic Committee—looking up at the sky where the clouds appear like whipped cream frosted onto a too-warm cake, porous and blotchy. I hear the sounds from the water underneath me, the pumping of the jets, the moving gurgles below.

The man in the next lap lane who sometimes flirts with me splashes his hand hard on the surface, like he is whacking someone's back in a hearty greeting at a bar where his friends have been meeting weekly for twenty-seven years. I imagine it is where they eat pizza sparse with pepperoni and sausage, drink tap beer, and complain about their wives or ex-wives a little too loudly but that the bartender is used to and the young waitresses ignore.

Swimming is a time I feel unburdened by responsibilities, relationships, deadlines, duties. It grants me pause from the running accounting and inventory of what I have done, what I have not done, and most pressingly, what I have yet to do.

HOPE

I HAVE FOUR MARY AND JOSEPH STATUES—NICE ONES TOO, not the cheap plastic ones like the solo monochromatic Josephs you bury in the front yard when you want to sell your house— but the porcelain kind that are graceful, artistic. Mary is always smiling; Joseph seems ambivalent, like he's posing for pictures.

The statues are not out on tables or sideboards for anyone to see and register my literal public display of Roman Catholicism but in the china cabinet on the top shelf, next to the tarnished silver pitcher and the vases I never use. Mary is facing me when I pass by. Sometimes I look at her. I wonder if she is always looking at me.

My late mother went to church every morning, a seven o'clock mass on her way to work, and then daily still when she retired. Going to church every week was nonnegotiable in our house growing up. Though you could occasionally claim a dispensation, we went to Mass on vacations every Sunday without fail, even when we were in a foreign country and didn't under-stand a word and only knew when it was the approximate time for Communion. You can stick your tongue out for a wafer in any language. Sometimes the wine is even good.

There is the hope that seems contained in the physical geog-raphy of Mass, the pureness of the gesture of suspending doubt and believing in the positive. There is the understanding that buoyed all the faithful throughout thousands of years of his-tory who fought for justice and fairness to move ahead in the name of hope, thanking God for each moment and each victory and each trial. That irrefutable and unwavering buy-in to all the mysteries and ambiguity.

And I have so enjoyed Mass; the songs and the rituals of standing and kneeling and sitting and standing and kneeling and sitting, a dance of devotion, the choreography playing out in churches all over the world every Sunday, every day, stretching across the planet. Or at least that is what the priests made you believe and why you donated every week to get more people on the planet in the same club. I was Catholic, we were Catholic; it was sewn into my identity.

I liked the idea that we all knew the same prayers in different languages. That we were all begging for forgiveness and mercy and asking for our specific calls to action. The Prayers of the Faithful. I was sure faithful. I am mostly still faithful.

I am mostly hopeful now.

I gathered from my lifetime embroidered in Catholicism that the goal was to try to live in the presence of grace, extracting it from the moments you could and seeing it where you could, acknowledging what extraordinary gifts you had been shown and trying never, ever, to diminish the worth of someone else. See the grace of God in everyone around you. Make something of your life by being good to others. Be someone who brings good to the world.

I believe in most of the essentials of what I learned at St. Luke's, Convent of the Sacred Heart, and weekly Mass—except the excessively judgmental parts, the corny early '70s part about boys bursting your bubble or becoming sterile if you sat on a cold gym floor, and also the part about unbaptized babies going to limbo; the God I spoke to loved children, he wouldn't do that.

I was raised on Catholic traditions that included but also went far beyond sending money to starving children and saving yourself for marriage.

Growing up, we said the Holy Rosary in our living room, all of us on our knees, every night after dinner. Sure, a lot of families said the "thanks for the grub" abbreviated version of prayer. But no one I knew did the whole Mother Teresa business—knees, rosary beads, scripture book in front of the picture window. It would help hold the family together, my mother said.

One Saturday night when Madeleine was sixteen and I was twelve, we were running late with saying the Rosary after dinner. Madeleine had a date at 7:30 and we were still in the middle of the Hail Marys when my father answered the door. He told the young man who was Madeleine's date to wait in the marble-floored foyer; the look on the boy's face frozen between panic and astonishment. Madeleine's hair was perfect after a stint with hot rollers; she wore shimmering blue eye shadow, mascara, and frosted lipstick that I borrowed often (a crime I always denied). In spite of Madeleine's beseeching whispers, my mother would not let her gracefully exit the Rosary.

To his credit, her date—a senior at a nearby all-boys Catholic high school—waited quietly for her in the front hall until the last Glory Be. After the conclusion of the petitions that thankfully had nothing to do with her, Madeleine rushed to grab her suede fringed purse from the kitchen. I am fairly certain he brought her home early.

We prayed out loud at home. We prayed in class at school. The nuns at St. Luke's were mostly kind, like Sister Lucy and Sister Lillian; but then there were the stern disciplinarians with the mean faces under their stark white-and-black habits, like

Sister Cecilia, the principal and the punitive fourth-grade nun we called Sister Tank.

The nuns at Sacred Heart where I went for middle school were a different breed—calmer, more sophisticated, elegant, refined. That could have been because it was an all-girls school. At Sacred Heart, we called the nuns Reverend Mother, and the top dog was Mother Superior; I liked that title: it was grand, regal, something to aspire to. I never wanted to be a nun, but I thought being a superior anything would be OK, especially a superior mother. I never took what any of them said literally nor did I go to the extreme in my interpretations. I liked the colorful metaphors and allegories. I loved the miracles—especially the loaves and fishes because I always felt that you could create abundance from scarcity and plainness. I knew it meant more than the fish, of course, and I tried every day to make more out of less.

For years attending Mass made me feel if not joyful, well, then, cleaner, like a rain shower rinse. It is permission to be there for an hour and think of nothing else than what is in front of me. And to feel small. In the space of the church with the vaulted ceilings and the chandeliers that must be hanging from fifty-foot metal chains glistening from the light of the stained-glass windows, the long pew-stacked aisles made for brides and First Communion dresses, I often felt my heartache was minimized.

I like that feeling of smallness, the way you are reduced when you stand on a beach alone and look out to the horizon to steady yourself, to put yourself in perspective. It doesn't have to be an ocean; I don't care if it's only a lake. You feel small. Like when you are in a forest on a hike.

Years ago, I was standing on a mesa in Sedona, Arizona; I had taken the boys for four days on a trip promised on a coupon to be at reduced cost if we sat through the pitch for a time-share. Weldon was thirteen, Brendan eleven, and Colin eight, and we took the Pink Jeep Tour because I'd found it online. A driver bounced our Jeep jerkily up to a mesa the color of rust, the color of lipstick. I stood there with my arms out and twirled and

I could see that the world was curved. That it was a circle. That I was small, and this was perfect.

The boys were just approaching or barely into their teen years, and I did not have a clue what was ahead. I do not know if anyone is fully prepared, braced for that collision course. But that day, that moment, in all the beauty that surrounded me—minus the Pink Jeep and the water bottles and the sweat under our sun hats—I felt hope for that day and the thousands upon thousands of days after. You could call it a moment of grace. And I am thankful for it, and all the millions of moments of grace that have flown into and out of my life on the coattails of hope.

I AM NOT AS REGULAR A CATHOLIC ANYMORE. I MISS THE regularity of attending weekly Mass sometimes. The singing mostly. There was a large part of my life, when I felt connection, fully formed as a Catholic, total buy-in. I believed prayers were answered, a call out and a return call. The halting of masses and large public gatherings at church for weddings, baptisms, and funerals in response to the global pandemic of 2020 only exacerbated the longing. Now no one could go.

The travesty of criminal assaults by priests who harmed generations of boys and girls was indeed silenced by the church. Acknowledging this legacy of betrayal, the healing is ongoing, and I see the injustices by perpetrators as separate from my larger beliefs. A reckoning is overdue.

Years ago I forced—and yes, it was by force—all three of my sons to attend Sunday school at St. Vincent Ferrer from kindergarten through eighth grade so they could be up-to-date on all their sacraments, like vaccinations against an evil world. They hated it, for different reasons, and Weldon spent some time in the dark hallway outside of the classroom each week because he questioned the volunteer teacher about the notion that heaven was for Catholics only and what exactly was the basis for the claim that it is the one true religion?

"What about Hindus? Jews? Buddhists? Episcopalians?" Weldon asked her.

The volunteer instructor was not amused and asked him to sit in the hall and think about it.

I agreed with him but told him to keep his Unitarianism to himself until confirmation. After that he was on his own. Just get the full sacraments under your belt, add the confirmation name, and you're fine.

Colin picked Anthony originally as his confirmation name because he said he always wanted to be called Tony. He was supposed to do research on the saint whose name he was assuming, but his was a shortcut.

"Tony. I want to be Tony."

Later he switched to Saint Dominic. He wanted to be Dom.

When he was in sixth grade, Brendan refused to go to Sunday school but then reversed his decision after my threat to take away the video controller.

His reason for not wanting to attend was that he already knew "the whole Mary."

"It's the Hail Mary," I reminded him.

My rationale for force-feeding them Catholicism—other than for the years when my mother was alive and we needed to meet her at mass every Sunday and sit together in the front pew—was that if they wanted to marry a Catholic, they needed to have all their sacraments in order.

As if Catholicism was the reason they would marry someone.

I married a Catholic and that didn't go well. I had my own marriage annulled, at my mother's insistence. Annulments are hard to come by these days, but this was 1996 and then it was pretty much just expensive, a few thousand dollars, and my mother paid for it. It was important to her that I have a clean Catholic slate. This is the magic of Catholic erasure. It didn't happen. The bishop said so.

The annulment process was a series of interviews by a layperson and his wife, plus a host of questions in about twenty pages of a questionnaire. I guess they wanted to get to the why. You can't be too careful erasing a marriage, you know, it has to be on certain grounds that the church finds acceptable.

The meetings—it would be harsh to call them interrogations—were in a church basement in another suburban parish after work in the evenings; I believe a plate of store-bought chocolate chip cookies and Styrofoam cups of coffee were involved.

There are eighteen canonical reasons you can get an annulment, and all of them are pretty juicy, including fear or force, but also error in judgment. I checked that one. And then about eleven more.

I got a certificate months later in the mail after they interviewed my ex-husband—who, for the record, was already remarried and objected to the annulment—but I guess you could predict that one too.

The annulment certificate is in a lockbox, along with my last will and testament where the boys get everything divided evenly, a third each. "Everything" is an inflated assessment of the leftovers. I will be working for many more years. I cannot afford to retire. There will not be much left over at all, I imagine, but they can fight over the furniture. I have put my sister Madeleine in charge of it all, and she will know what to do. I had the will drawn up years ago by a lawyer friend of my brother Paul's. As a single mother, I am relieved they are now older than the ages printed in the document with the provisions that as minors they would live with my brother Paul, who would raise them.

They are thirty-one, twenty-nine, and twenty-six now. So no need.

I DO LOVE THE CATHOLIC INVESTMENT IN HOPE. THE ELOQUENT expressions of pure love and devotion. The musings of Thomas Aquinas, the lessons of Saint Madeleine Sophie Barat. "Make prayer your delight; there find your rest and your happiness," was one of her quotes. Oh, if only it were that easy.

Before he died, Oliver Sacks, the physician and author of many books, possibly most memorable for me *The Man Who Mistook His Wife for a Hat*, wrote essays on his illness and dying in his final book, *Gratitude*. "I feel a sudden and clear focus and perspective. There is no time for anything inessential. I must focus on myself, my work and my friends. I shall no longer look at the NewsHour every night," he wrote.

I do not find it all that simple.

For my parents, it was faith that anchored them but also set them free.

I knew why my mother had the priests visit her in the hospital, then in extended care, then in hospice, and why she had her own plastic statue of Mary next to her bed with the guardrails. I could see in her eyes even in her final moments that she believed and it was righteous and I understood it then; but I am a little jealous now.

I go to the holiday masses, the weddings and the funerals and the baptisms, and I know the new prayers, but I guess they are not so new anymore, the Mass having a few years back undergone a makeover.

The recent update to the Mass was not as big a makeover as the switch from Latin to English. As a child I spent years thinking that "et cum *spiritu tuo*," the latter part of which I heard as "two-two-oh" was not the translation for "and the spirit with you" but the phone number of the church. I thought the priest conveniently announced it in the middle of Mass, just as in the commercials for the rug installation and the auto insurance. Just as with the Empire flooring company jingle, "five-eight-eight, two–three hundred, Empiiiiire."

Before the halt to public masses in response to the pandemic, my reason for not going to church every week was not because I am lazy but because sometimes I do not feel the hope as I wish I did. I have faith, but it is not fervent as it should be, as my parents' was. I feel at times like an observer, separated by a glass partition, as if I am watching myself perform as a Catholic behind a one-way mirror, the kind they have in interrogation rooms. Like I wasn't invited to the party but heard about it and just showed up, afraid to walk through the front door to where everyone else is having such a good time and has a plate of food on their laps filled with carefully made sandwiches and salads with the right amount of dressing. I sometimes feel like a fake. I find the homilies mostly inane.

Sometimes I experience despair, and I know it comes off as selfish and I know I have few squawky complaints in the scheme of the larger injustices of the world. Mine is a slipcovered life that looks neat and presentable on the outside but at times camouflages the disappointments, markings, and worn veneer beneath. I am this age, and my dreams for where I would be did not all happen, regardless of how hard I have tried. Sometimes I think that my mom would have been furious over my listless faith and she would remind me I need to be more grateful for every breath, every gift. That my life is easy, that I have countless blessings.

"Please help me," I say some nights to the air, to myself, to my pillow and every morning when I open my eyes in my lime-painted room with my paintings on the wall and the photos on my dresser of my sons, sisters, brothers, and close friends.

"Mary, help me."

But like everybody else in the whole world, I never really know what lies ahead that day or any other day, in spite of my planning and my doing and my deadlines and my bylines and my pay stubs, plus all the blue boxes on my Google calendar. And how dare I anyway.

I recently heard on the news that a woman walking down the street in downtown Chicago was instantly killed by a chunk of ice falling from a skyscraper. A child watching television on Christmas Day in her family's living room was shot in the head by a stray bullet from a passing car. A couple who were good friends and whose sons were friends with my boys were murdered in their home. A woman who lived near me was run over and killed as she was walking her dog. Cashiers at grocery stores and nurses in intensive care units died because they were infected with COVID-19 at work. Blacks are killed randomly and regularly by police.

I have felt for long stretches that nothing in life is neat except the knowledge that it is not neat. I do not think I have done anything to deserve this life—glorious or painful, highs or lows. It takes effort to be humble, to not succumb to the hubris that precedes a predictable doom. It takes effort to truly adhere to the notion that you are not in charge of any of this. That the luck can be haphazard and is not earned. That the distribution of blessings is inconsistent and unequal.

But I am someone who has clung to the notion that if you try harder, maybe just this next time, it will go as intended. From the smallest to the largest effort, I at times subscribed to that blind audacity.

Even though I have encountered random life events I had no control over, I am still the kind of person who turns her laptop on and off and on and off thirty-two times when something is amiss and I can of course fix it by myself. I am hoping that the next time will result in being able to properly download, attach, click, or whatever I need to happen that isn't happening.

On. Off. On. Off.

Nothing.

Yes, in the grander scheme, I want to be positive just as my father requested we be. Yes, I can act like I am having a good time because mostly, really most always, this is a good time. I want to house all the hope possible. I need the hope. I want to believe I am a half-full person full of myself like my mother wanted me to be.

But like everyone else, at times my life is littered with unplanned confetti bits of sorrow, shards of hurt, and sudden shocks that are hard to ignore. I know it is pointless and selfish to complain. I need the hope, the real hope, not the kind you wear like new narrow shoes that you end up taking off an hour in because they just don't feel right. Yes, Mom, I want to be full of myself. And I know that is different than getting over yourself. One is potential. The other is narrowing.

I want to resume the full-on Catholic part of me. Going to church is the least I can do for all I have been given, and for goodness sake, we now have Pope Francis, who believes we need to treat LGBTQ persons fairly and that our purpose is to end injustice. He even tweets—thoughtful, spiritual, eloquent messages, not stupid ones. And he apologizes when he makes mistakes. He is humble.

I want to feel what my mother and father never lost, never even questioned for a moment. I want the meaning, the inescapable belief, the faith that kept them afloat, the hope that no matter what, everything will be fine because it is in God's hands. I want to sustain that feeling you get with the Communion songs and the responsorial psalms and the recessional hymns you sing so loud the people in front of you turn around. My father's favorite hymn was "Eagle's Wings." When I hear it, I cry. Yes, I do believe God will hold me in the palm of his hand.

You have to go back to your life when Mass ends. But for that one hour you embody the hope because you sing the songs you know so well you feel like they are tattooed on your heart, and you say the prayers you have been muttering for a lifetime, and people you don't know smile at you and shake your hand just for the sake of it.

"Peace be with you."

"And also with you."

ACKNOWLEDGMENTS

My parents were good, loving people. I am so grateful to them for giving me the life I had and for a lifetime with my brothers and sisters, Mary Pat, Maureen, Bill, Madeleine, and Paul. I am also grateful to their spouses, Ken, Liz, Mike, and Diane.

My writing group friends, particularly my very dear ally Arlene Malinowksi, helped shape these essays over the past several years. Thanks to Elizabeth Berg, Veronica Chapa, Marja Mills, and Pamela Todd for listening and helping me edit, enhance, and delete. I rely on my journalism tribe of Alicia Shepard, Deborah Douglas, Teresa Puente, Katherine Lanpher, Angela Wright, Mary C. Curtis, Amy Guth, and Susy Schultz for their keen friendship as well as their wisdom on life and writing.

Dana Halsted, my dear, best friend of more than forty-five years, helps me see everything more clearly. Thanks to Sarah White, Swati Saxena, Sue Schmidt, Lisa Lauren, and Caryn Ward, who are forever supportive and offer up laughter and honesty. Diane Frisch, Julie Shelgren, Linda Berger, and Gail Galivan keep me connected to the past and present.

Thanks to Katie Orenstein for founding the OpEd Project, which for almost a decade has been a source of extraordinarily meaningful work. Thanks to Gloria Feldt for creating an organization where I have met inspiring leaders and gotten to tell their stories. I have had the luck and pleasure to work with talented friends Nailah Blades, Jovanka Ciares, Beth Terry, and Jennefer Witter.

My editor at Northwestern University Press, Jane Frances Bunker, was a joy to work with. Copy editor Lori Meek Schuldt made sure I was not in my own way and worked to make the manuscript the best it could be. I am grateful to the marketing team and am highly appreciative of the chance to be connected in another way to my alma mater.

I would not have the life I do without Weldon, Brendan, and Colin. I love you more.

I look forward to hearing from you with your comments or questions. Visit https://micheleweldon.com for updates on book signings, events, and more. You can also contact me at micheleweldon@msn.com or P.O. Box 5721, River Forest, IL 60305.

CREDITS

Chapter 4, "Dress Code," is adapted from Michele Weldon, "Stop Telling Women They're Too Old to Wear Something," NBC Think, August 25, 2018, https://www.nbcnews.com/think/opinion/stop-telling-women-they-re-too-old-wear-something-it-ncna902341. Reproduced with permission.

Chapter 6, "Negative Space," has excerpts from Michele Weldon, "Finding the Positive in Negative Space," *Pacific Standard*, May 29, 2019, https://psmag.com/.preview/cn02478 75820002481?auth=31d32a2bad780e7a008d2dd1446708b2611a a5ee&nonce=1558559509337. Reproduced with permission.

Chapter 8, "On Purpose," has excerpts from Michele Weldon, "Finding My Purpose: Is That All There Is?" Next Avenue, February 19, 2019, https://www.nextavenue.org/finding-my-purpose/. Reproduced with permission.

Chapter 15, "Lap Lanes," is adapted from Michele Weldon, "I Go Swimming to Try to Forget That I'm Dying," NBC Think, October 6, 2019, https://www.nbcnews.com/think/opinion/i-go-swimming-try-forget-i-m-dying-then-i-ncna1051671. Reproduced with permission.